Praise for *How to Tell a Naked*

"Discover everything you need to know to create a special, sexy night for you and your man—as well as setting the foundation for a long-term, healthy erotic relationship . . . get ready to rock that bed like never before!"

—*Complete Woman*

"What sets her book apart is Royalle's warm, down-to-earth voice. Her tone is literally the opposite of brazen, but the information is still bold . . . and empowering—and she puts women's pleasure first."

—*The Village Voice*

"*How to Tell a Naked Man What to Do* will leave you filled with inspiration on how to make your wants the principle when it comes to pleasure."

—*Bust*

"Candida Royalle's knowledge on sex and relationships is invaluable. If you're not getting what you need out of your sex life, this book is a must-read! Find out how to ask for what you want and set the stage for incredible lovemaking."

—Veronica Hart, adult film director and actor

"Sassy, smart, sexy, and secure, Candida Royalle is a pioneer filmmaker who knows what women want erotically—there's no single greater talent to tell a woman how to maximize her sexual potential with a lover."

—Dr. Patti Britton, sex coach and coauthor of *The Complete Idiot's Guide to Sensual Massage*

HOW
TO TELL
A
NAKED
MAN
WHAT
TO DO

SEX ADVICE FROM A
WOMAN WHO KNOWS

Candida Royalle

A FIRESIDE BOOK
PUBLISHED BY SIMON & SCHUSTER
NEW YORK   LONDON   TORONTO   SYDNEY

FIRESIDE
Rockefeller Center
1230 Avenue of the Americas
New York, NY 10020

This Fireside Edition 2006

For information regarding special discounts for bulk purchases, please contact
Simon & Schuster Special Sales at 1-800-456-6798 or
business@simonandschuster.com.

Designed by Chris Welch

Manufactured in the United States of America

1   3   5   7   9   10   8   6   4   2

The Library of Congress has catalogued the hardcover edition as follows:
How to tell a naked man what to do : sex advice from a woman who knows / Candida Royalle.
      p.   cm.
Includes index.
1. Sex instruction for women. I. Title
HQ46.R69 2004
613.9'6—dc22   2004053244
ISBN-13: 978-0-7432-5530-1
ISBN-10: 0-7432-5530-5
ISBN 13: 978-0-7432-6645-1 (Pbk.)
ISBN-10: 0-7432-6645-5 (Pbk.)

This book is dedicated to Linda Hirsch, C.S.W., without whose brilliant and compassionate guidance I would not have arrived at this place in my life.

Contents

Introduction

Who would have thought that one day I would make a career out of telling naked men what to do? My childhood was as normal as anybody else's. I was raised in a middle-class home, with a big Italian family on one side and an Irish Catholic family on the other. I joined the Brownies and then the Girl Scouts, took dance lessons, and waited until I fell in love and turned eighteen to "go all the way." Why, I didn't even have my first orgasm until I was nineteen! Yes, there was some unconventionality: my dad was a professional jazz drummer, and both my sister and I were educated in special schools for artistic kids in Manhattan. But when it came to sex, aside from some innocent sensual touching between me and a girlfriend in our early teens, I was as naive and inexperienced as the next girl.

Perhaps the road I eventually took in my adult life had its genesis in the conflict between my blossoming sexuality and a growing fear of sex as dangerous and uncontrollable. My family wasn't that comfortable with sex, and I, like most young girls at that time, received absolutely no sex education other than to "just say no!" When I was thirteen, I was sexually assaulted in a park, and though I miraculously managed to fight off my attacker and avoid being raped, the psychological damage had been done: I had convinced myself that *my* sexuality was the reason for the attack. The message I internalized was that my sexual urges must be contained or, if let loose, they would cause men to do terrible things to me. Despite all of this, I still somehow managed to develop a tremendous appetite for sexual pleasure.

We all cope with our personal conflicts differently. My way was to throw myself completely into sexual experimentation with total abandon and at times even recklessness. When I moved to San Francisco at age twenty-one, I experimented with drugs and recreational sex to my heart's and body's content. I performed in avant-garde theater, worked on and sold my art, and sang in jazz clubs. But I soon discovered that I needed a way to finance my unconventional lifestyle. That's when I answered an ad for nude modeling—only the agent had other ideas. He decided I would be perfect for porn movies, and I stormed out of his office in a huff. But when my then boyfriend decided to try his hand (and other parts!) at being a porn stud, his experience led me to reconsider the offer. After he landed a much coveted leading role in a film called *Cry for Cindy* for one of the better adult film directors of the time, Anthony Spinelli, I took the opportunity to visit the film set and get a better look at what the adult industry was all about. I, like most people, presumed it was a sleazy underworld filled with greasy directors and pitiful drug addicts who needed money for their next fix. To my surprise, what I discovered was a clean and professional environment, a legitimate industry filled with Hollywood types moonlighting on porn crews for extra cash, and intimidatingly gorgeous young women and men competing for roles. This was the "boogie nights" era that gave rise to the big-budget porn classics that were shot on film and played in venues like the long-gone Pussycat Theatre. Gerard Damiano's groundbreaking flick *Deep Throat* put plot and humor into porn, and his atmospheric classic *The Devil in Miss Jones*, starring the exceptional Georgina Spelvin, proved you could make a movie that was compelling *and* sexually explicit. Suddenly it was appealingly risqué for couples to frequent the big triple-X movie theaters and there was something cutting edge, almost hip, about daring to bare it all in front of the camera.

Given the alternative lifestyle I was living in San Francisco, where breaking taboos was an everyday part of the gender-bending, sexual experimentation, anything-goes mindset of that time, jumping over to perform in sexually explicit films suddenly didn't feel like such a leap, so I began appearing in films. It was easy, I could make a lot of money in a short period of time, and it afforded me the ability to focus on my other artistic pursuits that were less lucrative.

I was an active feminist and reasoned that it was my body to do with what I wanted. After all, the women's movement was all about choice: Some women may choose to cast off their aprons and don a suit and join the corporate world. Others may keep their aprons and work at home. I chose to cast off everything and use my looks, my body, my open attitude toward sex, and my healthy sexual appetite to make a living.

I easily landed roles in some of the bigger features, performing and forming friendships with many of the stars of that time, including Annette Haven, Leslie Bovee, Samantha Fox, John Leslie, Paul Thomas, and the most infamous, John Holmes. Even though I was a bit shy about appearing naked on screen (I was never fully convinced I had a good enough body) and not completely comfortable with the often crude depiction of sex in most mainstream porn movies, I became a sought-after actress for my ability to learn lines and deliver them somewhat convincingly. And, contrary to what people say about the adult film world, I was never forced or coerced to do anything. In fact we were given lists to check off, specifying what we would and wouldn't consent to do on screen.

I made about five or six features a year for five years. My experiences were mostly good as long as I worked with directors who took pride in what they were doing, and I avoided the sleazebags who were contemptuous of their casts.

However, over time the gnawing ambivalence about what I was doing caught up with me. I truly felt it was perfectly fine to perform sexually for consenting adults to view and enjoy. But at the same time, I was reticent to tell anyone outside my inner circle what I did to earn money. It became clear to me that I needed to stop making light of what I was doing and take a closer look at my feelings about it.

In the end, I decided to end my career as a porn star and move on to other pursuits. But I gave myself one last year to make movies I could be proud of, including Henri Pachard's *October Silk*, Chuck Vincent's *Fascination, Delicious,* and my swan song, *Blue Magic,* which I wrote, foreshadowing things to come. During the last year I met and married my (now ex-) husband, moved back to my native New York City, and started writing for men's magazines. I also found a remarkable therapist with whom I unraveled the complex issues surrounding my foray into porn. What exactly *is* wrong with making love for others to view and enjoy? Do explicit movies make men go out and do bad things to women? Should I feel ashamed of having performed in them?

Reassessing my own attitudes and coming to terms with my scarlet past ultimately led me to examine the vast terrain of hypocrisy and sexual fear. How did we go from worshipping the goddess Aphrodite, who embodied female sexual power, to teaching generations of women that sex was to be tolerated, a duty to be performed in the interest of providing children and favors to their husbands?

Sexual desire is one of our most primary and wonderful gifts, yet we are still fighting over what kind of sex is acceptable, where, why, and with whom. We use sex to sell anything and everything possible, from computers to cars to kitchen appliances, yet it is still considered immoral to look at humans engaging in real, honest-to-goodness sex.

The more I contemplated these apparent contradictions, the more I came to feel that what we really need as a society is an honest way to look at and feel good about our sexuality. Contrary to all the cautionary tales and moral judgments, the desire to view sexually explicit imagery is a natural human curiosity. Rather than pornography causing us to act out in certain ways, I saw contemporary pornography as a reflection of the society that created it. Were women in fact exploited? Yes. Women were essential to the creation and sales of commercial porn, and yet their sexuality was completely ignored and misrepresented.

I began to wonder what it would be like to create explicit movies that give us good information about sex while entertaining and inspiring us. Could I create movies that accurately reflected female desire, movies that women and men could enjoy together? I *didn't* like a lot of what I saw in contemporary porn, but rather than march around waving banners of protest, I decided to put my money where my mouth is and try to produce adult movies that make us feel good about ourselves. After all, people are not going to stop looking at sex, and if women don't take control of the means of production, men will continue to do it for us, continuing to erroneously define female sexuality.

If women are to experience the sexual pleasure that is our right, it is incumbent upon us to challenge the plethora of negative messages thrown our way and toss them aside. I believe there's an underlying fear in our culture, thousands of years old, that if we women were to discover just how powerful our sexuality is, we'd abandon our families and run wild in the streets! As the late Dr. William Masters of Masters and Johnson said when describing the findings of his early research, "Women's capacity for pleasure would put any man to shame." And if we keep ourselves wrapped up in guilt and shame and the fear of being exposed as "too experienced," we'll never know the pleasure that we are capable of. The really silly part is that our relationships and our marriages would probably fare way better, and divorce rates plummet, if women *did* come to the bedroom fully informed and equal participants. After all, one of the biggest causes of marital woes is boredom in the bedroom. Put two people together who are comfortable with their own individual sexuality and eager to explore, and you're a lot less likely to see that unwelcome guest called boredom settling into bed with you.

Hence, Candida Royalle, director of erotic movies from a woman's point of view, was born.

I've now made fifteen films, and thousands of women and men write to me all the time to say how much they enjoy seeing real women having good sex on screen. Their responses have been particularly gratifying for me, since creating material that makes women feel good about themselves and their desires and gives them permission to explore their sexuality—guilt free—has been the ultimate goal of my efforts. As one young woman in her twenties told me some time ago, "Watching your movies made me feel comfortable with my own sexual desires." And in case you're one of those who think men aren't receptive to this newer vision of female-centric erotica, I've gotten many letters from men over the years, including one who wrote, "I am touched by the sensitivity that you put in your films, which convey the difference between sheer sex and making love, as well as showing affection for the individual that you make love with. I, for one, am very happy that there is a person such as yourself out there who can give viewers of adult films a broader choice of what they can watch."

Now I would like to share all that I've learned with you. Through my director's lens, I have created a book that reads like a film: In one sitting a woman can discover all she needs to know to become a sensual, mindful lover, one who is in touch with her own sexuality as well as the ways she can communicate this knowledge to her man. Just as a director puts together an entertaining, enjoyable film, so too must a woman take charge of her own sexual pleasure. The chapters mirror the process of preparing for and enacting a night of stellar lovemaking—beginning with getting in touch with the inner you, moving through the shoot in which you and your lover play out the script of your fantasies, and ending with the erotic exchange between you and your lover as you revisit your steamy night in scintillating detail. I've also included many entertaining "Director's Notes" and Tricks of the Trade to inspire your sex life.

My journey toward personal acceptance and sexual self-knowledge has been a long and unusual one. I have gone from innocence to taboo, from college feminist to porn star. I spent my twenties having as many one-night stands as I wished and my thirties being a good monogamous wife. I've experienced some of the most mind-blowing sex you can imagine, but not before having to confront psychological fears that interfered with my ability to experience the rich passionate sexuality that was mine. Not all of us have to break taboos and confront painful demons in order to experience the rich and unique sexuality that is ours. All you really need is the desire and a willingness to open yourself up to being creative and having fun. And I've learned that when all is said and done, having fun is what it's all about.

Phase One

Research

Chapter 1

Undress Your Mind

The word *normal* should never be used in the
context of sex.
—Dr. Marty Klein, psychotherapist and sexual educator

Even before the preproduction stage of producing a film, I go
through what I call a "research phase," during which I sit
down and clarify exactly what I want to say in my movie.
What aspects of sexual experience do I want to explore? And ultimately, what message about sexuality do I want my movie to deliver? Most people probably assume that producing an adult movie
does not require a lot of thought—after all, the most obvious feature of my films is their visual and dramatic explicitness. But I see
anything I do—whether it be directing a movie or writing an article or a book—as a way of conveying some idea to the viewer or
the reader; I want the film to have a purpose. I recall reading an interview with the director Ingmar Bergman, in which he said, "If
you have nothing to say, you shouldn't make a movie." I imagine
we'd have a lot fewer movies and a lot less schlock on the video
shelves if everyone adhered to that message.

In my films, I believe in providing not just a turn-on, which of course is the most important thing in terms of an adult movie, but also useful information that women and men can apply to their personal lives, whether it be some nugget of wisdom I've learned about relationships or a great sex tip. The best example of my approach is captured in my movie *Bridal Shower*, in which a group of women friends at a bridal shower share stories about how they got their men to understand their sexual needs and give them what they want in bed. These secrets were all culled from my own life, so I knew they worked. I dramatized such advice as helping a new beau get over his performance anxiety by using the "give-and-get" method developed by Masters and Johnson or trying to get a new lover to slow down and be more sensual along the way to being sexual. But sometimes a film doesn't require a heavy message or instructive information, and I decide that what my viewers might really enjoy is some laughter and excitement—after all, where would our sex lives be if we didn't have a sense of humor?! One such film, *One Size Fits All*, has absolutely no message, but it offers a fun story filled with good humor and great hot sex. My most recent film, *Stud Hunters*, is a spoof about a woman erotic filmmaker searching for some hot new studs for her next movie.

A SIMPLE AND BRIEF DESCRIPTION OF THE GIVE-AND-GET METHOD

Decide at the outset of lovemaking that you are *not* going to have intercourse—and stick to it! Then as you proceed to kiss, touch, fondle, once your man has gotten an erection, stop everything and let it go down until he's completely flaccid. Then start all over again. While this may not seem like fun to him, the point is, he will realize he can achieve an erection at will, over and over and over. By agreeing you will not engage in intercourse, the pressure to perform is removed from him and he's more likely to get an erection. When I tried this on my past lover he wasn't thrilled at the prospect. But it worked like a charm. He came to understand that it was only his anxiety that was getting in the way and not a real problem of his getting and maintaining an erection.

If your guy is still having difficulty, you may need more professional counseling to help him with whatever is going on. See my resource list at the end of the book for counselors in your area.

No matter what I decide to say through my movies, the point is that I must first do some research so that I know—going into pre-production—what I want to offer my audience. Do I want my audience to sit back, relax, and enjoy themselves while they watch a rollicking comedy? Or do I want to give them an opportunity to expand their sexual horizons, by showing them some wild new techniques for getting it on with their lover? Just like audiences want different films for different moods, they also want different types of sex for their different moods.

WHAT TYPE OF SEX ARE YOU IN THE MOOD FOR?

Our moods vary daily, monthly, even yearly. Why wouldn't our mood for sex change with our overall state of mind? I've found that women want different types of sex for different moods. Consider these moods and the corresponding type of sex:

- If you're in a quiet mood, try sex with no words. Ever noticed how sexy it can be when you can't make noise? Pretend you're still living at home with Mom and Dad and you can't make a peep.
- If you're in a lazy mood, you might enjoy slow, dreamy sex with a lot of touching, kissing, and fondling. Maybe even decide *not* to engage in full-blown intercourse.

○ If you're in a tense mood, take that energy and put it into some fast, hot sex. Try out one of those gotta-have-it role-playing fantasies where one of you takes the other.

○ If you're in a spicy mood, add some toys to your lovemaking. Take a trip together to your local erotic shop or Web site, or surprise him with something. Try something new that you've been thinking about.

As a director, I need to know what I'm trying to achieve going into preproduction. This same rule applies to preparing for a night of lovemaking with your partner: you need to do some research and get in touch with what kind of scenario you want to create with your lover. What sort of lovemaking do you want to engage in? Are there particular fantasies you've longed to share and play with? Have you always dreamed of playing the sexy high-priced call girl? Or the innocent virgin? Do you secretly long to be tied up? Or to tie *him* up? Do you even know what your private fantasies are? What pushes your buttons? Do you know what pushes his buttons? Are you afraid of what you find when you close your eyes and begin to fantasize? These are some of the research questions every woman needs to ask herself in order to prepare for a night of steamy sex, one that could lead into an even hotter, sexier relationship. Sometimes it's necessary to peer into our own psyches and make sure we're ready for the ecstasy we're craving. Are we ready and able to experience the pleasure we seek? Are there some inhibitions hiding in the recesses of our minds that might get in the way of truly enjoying our dream lover? Do we even know what we want sexually?

In the following pages, I will suggest a few ways you can begin to undress your sexual star. I will also point out some of the more common obstacles that may be getting in the way of you fully accessing the pleasure you seek. These tips and advice will help you through your research phase. Remember, the better you know your inner sexual star the better prepared you'll be and the more pleasure you will experience.

Get to Know Your Inner Star

The best sex is between two people who come to the bedroom fully informed about their own needs and desires. They know what gets them off and how they like to be touched and where. You're not going to get very far if either of you thinks the other should just know what you want. So it's up to you to make sure you do know what you like, and then communicate those desires to your lover. The more you are in touch with what gets you hot, the better you will be able to show your lover how to please you. The tired idea that "good girls" should not know about things sexual and wait for their men to teach them sent a lot of women into marriages and relationships completely naive and expecting the man to magically know everything. The result was all too often an unhappy couple with a terribly dysfunctional sex life. No wonder men often develop performance anxiety! What a burden to have to know everything about someone you're just becoming intimate with. It's impossible! So how do you get to know what you want and what turns you on? There are three simple ways to approach getting to know yourself better: 1) know the role of your own body; 2) open yourself to learning how to be fully sensual; and 3) investigate self-pleasuring.

Know the Role of Your Body

When I fell in love and got together with my very first boyfriend, I was disappointed to discover that after making love—for minutes or hours—I always felt a little frustrated. It was as if my body was still craving some unknown attention that had not yet been met. It wasn't until I read *Our Bodies, Ourselves* and learned about the specifics of my anatomy down there, that I understood what I had been missing. The more I examined the details of my own genitalia, the more I understood what happens when I become sexually excited. For instance, before I began my investigation, I thought that I was abnormal if I didn't have an orgasm during intercourse. Nothing could be further from the truth. I soon learned that most women need clitoral stimulation to orgasm. The more I learned, the more I could direct myself *and* my lover. I have spoken with a number of women who have shared similar stories about how naive they were as young women about their intimate knowledge of their own bodies. One woman remembers having frequent sex with her first boyfriend (in the back of his Chevy no less) throughout her twenties. "I did not have one orgasm. And I had no idea how to have one. It wasn't until I met my future husband, who showed me how to touch myself, that I finally began to explore my own body and what it wanted."

Here are some tips on getting to know your anatomy—firsthand:

1. Consult the beautiful and detailed diagrams in either the recently updated *Our Bodies, Ourselves,* or Betty Dodson's *Sex for One: The Joy of Selfloving* or *Orgasms for Two: The Joy of Partnersex,* which has a wealth of great information.
2. Take a mirror and do a self-exam. I know some of you may feel uncomfortable peering at or into yourselves, but such investigation is all part of your larger journey to knowing what you want and how to get it. With the mirror's help, become more familiar with your labia—inner and outer—as well as your clitoris.
3. Discover how to find your own G-spot. This advice comes courtesy of Dr. Beverly Whipple, the noted researcher who helped to discover the now famous G-spot: squat down and insert one or two fingers into your vagina with your palm facing up. Gently

touch the upper part of the vaginal wall and try to feel a dime-sized area that is ridgy, rather than smooth. Keep in mind that some women have an easy time finding their sacred spot, while others have no luck at all. In fact, many women claim not to have one, and there are those who even question whether the infamous G-spot really exists. There are some terrific videos that explore the G spot and direct women how to find theirs. (See my resource list.) But don't feel pressured. We're not all built the same way!

Open Yourself Sensually

An important way to know and understand yourself sexually is by becoming more sensual with yourself. Just as in partner sex, where we often rush past the more subtle, sensuous aspects of lovemaking, we also tend to skip over our own sensual potential. As I mentioned earlier, I often use my movies to share the lessons I've learned about life, love, and especially sex. An example of this is in my movie *Eyes of Desire, Part One*. The lead, Lisa, is experiencing something of a sexual awakening after being intrigued with a mystery man. At one point in the movie she lowers herself into a warm bath and begins to sensuously caress her whole body, taking some time before her hands find their way down to her genitals. We can almost feel what she's feeling as she glides her hands along her wet silky skin, while we're voyeuristically enjoying the pleasure she's obviously feeling.

I have put other such sensual scenes in several of my movies because I have learned how pleasurable it is to caress myself all over and I want to encourage women to do this for themselves as a way to further know themselves sexually—it's sort of like sensate focus for one. Sensate focus (which is described in detail in chapter 10) is a tool suggested by therapists for couples who have lost the spark in their sexual relationship. Essentially, it's about relearning how to touch and respond to or receive such touch. Most of us, after years of making love, forget the pleasures of a soft caress as we race to the genitals in our goal-oriented approach to lovemaking. Sensate focus is a way of slowing down and reawakening the multitude of sensations available to us through tender touching and stroking. We forget that the entire body is an erogenous zone, and that the skin is amazingly sensitive.

In my movie *Three Daughters,* I wanted to convey the splendor of a young woman who first begins to open herself to the full range of her sensuality. In the film, I try to capture how a young woman experiences pleasure when she experiments with one of her girlfriends. We then watch Heather meet and develop a relationship with the man who will be her first lover.

I never like to put scenes between women in my Femme Productions movies just for the sole purpose of titillating men with the age-old fantasy of watching two women together. I don't begrudge them that, but because my work is specifically aimed at women's fantasies, I am sensitive to the fact that while many women are extremely turned on by the idea of sex with another female, some are equally turned off. I reserve scenes between women for scripts where it has a purpose and between actresses who truly are lesbians or bisexual. In *Three Daughters,* since it was about a young woman's sexual blossoming, I wanted to portray something that happened to me in my early sexual development and something that is quite common between young women: the sensual exploration of bodies between girlfriends.

While Heather and her friend are eighteen and older, this occurred for me when I was only thirteen, which is actually a more common age for such typical sensual exploration. My friend and I studied ballet and loved to practice together at home. It all started innocently enough. We'd put on music and dance expressively around the living room. But eventually we began to play a game whereby one of us would take turns being the guy. Whoever played the guy would slowly remove the other's clothes and then proceed to sensuously caress her body from head to toe. My memory makes it seem like this went on for hours and maybe it did. I recall it feeling incredible and like nothing I had ever experienced before. Because we were so virginal (I already loved boys and had had a steady boyfriend, but had never done more than kiss), our sensuous game never got genital. It remained completely sensuous and focused on the body, never nearing the genitalia at all.

In *Three Daughters,* Heather and her friend go further. After all, they were over eighteen and this *is* an adult movie! But in my case, I marvel at the fact that we played with such feelings at that age. In hindsight, this was perhaps the most determining factor in my sexual development and in terms of the kind of lover I would become as well as seek out. I believe this little innocent game she and I played taught me more about sensuality and good sex than anything I've ever learned since. In fact, as I'll talk about later on, at a certain point in my adult life, I had to make a conscious effort to get back those incredible feelings of sensuality that at one time came so naturally to me. Incidentally, the American Association of Sex Educators, Counselors, and Therapists (AASECT) selected *Three Daughters* for a special screening at one of its national conferences due to its "positive sexual role modeling."

One of my favorite things in the morning when I wake up is to caress my body. I put a lot of effort into keeping my skin soft and supple. Lying in bed in those first moments of the day when my senses are most alive and refreshed gives me an opportunity to caress myself and appreciate the results of all that effort. Not only does it feel good to run my hands along my body, I'm also amazed at the softness of my belly and the smoothness of my thighs. I feel confident presenting myself to my lover and motivated to keep up my personal beauty regimen (which I go deeper into in chapter 8).

CANDIDA CLOSE-UP

Q: When I'm alone I can masturbate to the point of having wonderful orgasms. However, during sex I have never been able to have one. I've tried using my fingers but the sensations that I get from a vibrator are much stronger. Oral sex also does not help me come. Do you have any suggestions? This is very frustrating.

A: It often happens that the way we learn to masturbate remains the best and sometimes only way we can come. So why not just pull out your trusty vibrator during sex play with your partner? Some women are self-conscious about masturbating in front of their lover or pulling out their favorite sex toy, but if the guy is confident in himself and in your desire for him, he's usually happy to help you with whatever it takes. The creative part is coming up with a way to make him feel included. Show him how to hold it on you, or let him put his fingers inside you and do some exploring while you use the vibrator on yourself, which can take your orgasms to an even greater height by stimulating the G-spot. If you'd like to explore other ways to climax, you can always consult a sex therapist who might be able to introduce you to new sensations by teaching you a process called "sensate focus" where you spend time with your lover just touching and rediscovering sensations you'd forgotten. But if you're happy with your vibrator and your lover doesn't feel left out, bring it on out. As long as you're both getting satisfaction together, who cares how it's achieved?

Self-Pleasuring

There's nothing like self-pleasuring to find out exactly what images are running through your erotic mind and what you need in order to feel pleasure and climax. Simply close your eyes and begin to caress yourself all over your body and eventually on your genitals. As you roam your body, stay open to what images and scenarios begin to enter your mind. Go with them, don't edit them, and see where they go. These are your personal fantasies, the thoughts and images that turn you on.

Next, pay attention to how you're touching yourself. What feels good to you? Do you like sensuously caressing your breasts? Your belly? And how do you like to stimulate yourself? Do you require direct clitoral stimulation? Do you like to have something inside of your vagina? Do you like it hard? Fast? Soft or slow? Do you prefer the soft flesh of your fingers or do you like a hard vibrating object?

You might want to try playing around with some sex toys. Vibrators, dildos, and other sexual enhancers allow women to pleasure themselves as they learn exactly how they like to be touched, and what depth or angle of penetration is most stimulating. By using toys, you can do such inquiry in privacy, without worrying about your lover. Once you've mastered masturbation, you'll be able to tutor your lover as to how to best please you.

And remember to take your time and be sensuous with yourself. Several years ago after a particularly painful breakup I went to a masturbation workshop given by Annie Sprinkle and Joe Kramer. They talked about taking the emphasis off of our genitals and turning the act of simple masturbation into a ritualistic session of self-love. They suggested lighting candles, burning incense, wearing something sensual, and sitting in front of a mirror as you make love to yourself the way you would to someone else. I liked this both because it helped me stay focused on good feelings as I healed from the breakup, and because it taught me to be more sensuous with myself. Just as in making love with a partner, self-pleasuring doesn't have to be a race toward the genitals and a quick and forgettable orgasm. Taking the time to appreciate the softness of our skin and the subtleties of our arousal can awaken in us feelings we never knew we were capable of and turn us into far more sensuous lovers.

TEACHING *HIM* YOUR ANATOMY

Knowing your own anatomy is only the first step in making sure you get what you need. The second step is teaching *him* your anatomy. This isn't always easy, because many women feel a little awkward playing show-and-tell down there. If you feel comfortable, the easiest way to accomplish this little lesson is to take a mirror and guide him around your personal attributes by saying, "Here's my outer labia, here's my inner labia, say hi to my little clitty . . ." You could even turn the moment into a fun warm-up fantasy game and play teacher and student.

Another way you can help him get to know you better is to show him one of those anatomical diagrams in *Our Bodies, Ourselves*, or the beautiful renderings in Dr. Betty Dodson's first book, *Sex for One*, that show the fascinating variety of lovely vulvas among us women. Looking at pictures together may lead the two of you into faraway places.

Perhaps the most effective way to accomplish the task at hand is to guide him around your anatomy while expressing what feels good as he's exploring and trying to please you. Most partners genuinely want to find out what works and appreciate knowing what they're doing right and how to do it even better. An episode from *Sex and the City* comes to mind here. Samantha (naturally!) has just finished reading the book *The Clitoral Truth* by Rebecca Chalk, and is explaining to her boyfriend exactly how to use his fingers as he's manually stimulating her. "Take your middle finger and reach up just inside. Do you feel that little area on top with the ridges? That's it. Now take your thumb and place it on my clitoris. Yes, that's it, a little lower, a little harder, that's it . . ." Need I say more? Direction is in the detail!

Once we realize that a good lover *wants* direction and we get over our shyness about telling a man exactly how we like to be touched, our sexual pleasure and satisfaction can only get better and better.

CANDIDA CLOSE-UP

Q: I am wondering if it is possible to teach myself to have an orgasm. I have been having sex for eight years now, and have never had an orgasm. I am a female, in good health, and my doctor has assured me that there is no physical reason for my problem.

A: It is indeed possible to teach yourself how to have an orgasm. The first thing I would ask you is if you masturbate. Masturbating helps a woman discover how she likes to be touched, what sort of physical stimulation she needs to have an orgasm, and what sorts of fantasies can help her get to that level of excitement. Reading sexy books or looking at sexy movies (like my Femme line!) can help you get in touch with your fantasies. The Sinclair Intimacy Institute has a wonderful video called *Becoming Orgasmic;* there are some terrific edutainment titles that address female pleasure, like the beautiful *Secrets of Female Sexual Ecstasy,* distributed by Pacific Media Entertainment; and finally, Dr. Betty Dodson, considered the "mother of masturbation," has a wonderful line of books and videos that teach women how to masturbate and self-pleasure themselves.

If these don't help, I would strongly advise you to find a good therapist or counselor. There can be many hidden emotional or psychological reasons for not being able to have an orgasm, such as growing up in a home that strongly frowned upon sexual pleasure or early childhood trauma. Talking to a counselor whom you trust can help you discover what might be holding you back. One good source is the American Association of Sex Educators, Counselors, and Therapists (AASECT) at www.aasect.org. They can help you locate someone in your area.

Stage Fright

Sometimes knowing what you like is not enough if you're suffering from inhibitions. These inhibitions can stem from discomfort about your body, embarrassment about your fantasies, or a shamefulness about what you like to do sexually. I recall one of my close girlhood friends who had inherited her mother's large, voluminous breasts—as well as her mother's terrible discomfort with them. We would giggle over the fact that her mother would always wear a bra to bed, but as my girlfriend's breasts filled out, she too began trying to camouflage them with loose-fitting sweaters and a hunched-over posture. Many women would be envious of such round, luscious breasts, but she had grown up with a mother who set an example of being uncomfortable with what she had, and came of age at a time when the fashion model Twiggy was all the rage and it was suddenly fashionable to look more like a young boy than a woman. Once she began dating and acquired her first boyfriend her discomfort with her breasts caused her to be terribly inhibited. She would only make love with the lights off and often refused to remove her bra. Over time, and with the gentle coaxing and loving support of her beau, she got over her inhibitions and was able to accept her bountiful breasts, as well as make love with the lights on. My friend's story is not dissimilar to that of many women in that she internalized shame about her body. Let's take a look at what's behind our body image and other inhibiting factors.

Body Image

Let's talk about body image first. As we saw with my childhood friend, a poor body image can really inhibit you from completely letting go and giving yourself over to the pleasure you could be feeling. If we're too busy worrying about whether our breasts are perky enough or our bellies look too round, we're being distracted from the delicious feelings we could be experiencing with our partner. If you ask a man what turns him on most about a woman he's making love to, he'll more often than not tell you it's seeing her excited and lost in the pleasure. He's certainly not thinking about the size of your thighs or the shape of your breasts. He's completely into the woman who is so into him. But many women are often cut off from this kind of abandon because they are concerned or distracted by a poor body image or worries about whether they smell good or not. I know—it's very difficult not to think about how we look in a bathing suit, never mind naked, but when we get too absorbed in *how we look*, we lose our ability to know *how we feel*, which is so much more important to having great sex.

While it's not always easy to simply begin to like yourself after years of self-doubt or not taking care of yourself, it's important to realize that we are much more critical of our bodies than men are. Men are looking for excitement in a woman and the feeling that they are able to help create this excitement. They're not sitting there with a checklist of our pluses and minuses; they're looking for us to have good, lusty fun with them—and that does not require a perfect body. As much as we are bombarded by Hollywood movies and fashion magazines that feature unattainable images of beauty and perfection, we really *don't* have to be perfect and reed thin to be lovable and desirable. What we need is to feel good about ourselves and comfortable with our sexuality. A woman who feels good will also feel sexy, and a woman who feels sexy *is* sexy.

Sometimes we use our weight and body image as a way of not connecting to others out of some deep, subconscious fear of giving ourselves to another. Perhaps every time you begin to get close to someone you start to put on weight again and withdraw. There could be many reasons for this: fear of having our hearts broken, or a history of childhood abuse that we may or may not even be aware of. If you sense this may be true for you, it might be wise to seek out professional counseling. These problems and issues are treatable as long as you're willing.

Yet many if not most of us find true love and lust and happiness. Yes, we should all ideally watch our weight by eating a healthy diet and working out regularly. But there are ways for all of us to look desirable no matter our size or shape. (I'll talk more about the use of lingerie and lighting to enhance our bodies in chapters 5 and 6.) As my friend Dr. Diana Wiley likes to point out, the important lesson to learn is how to embrace our unique selves, our differences, our quirky individualities, and see ourselves as those who love us see us and to see those very unique and quirky differences as endearing and lovable. Another reward for all of that is that the more accepting we learn to be of ourselves, the more accepting we become of others, especially our partners, and that makes for some very positive loving.

DIRECTOR'S NOTE

Women are much more critical of their bodies than men. Men are turned on more by a woman getting into sex than they are by a woman with a size six body without cellulite.

As for your own particular scent, it's equally important to feel comfortable about how you smell, and sometimes this is not so easy. With all the ads for perfumes and douches and deodorants, we certainly grow up with a lot of negative messages about our personal odors. We seem to have forgotten that those very odors are the signals we send out to our potential lovers; these scents and "pheromones" are said by experts to be picked up by potential lovers at a subliminal level, helping to create sexual attraction and desire. If you want to feel confident about how you smell, the wisest thing to do would be to eat a healthy diet rich in fruits and vegetables and drink lots of plain water. We are, after all, what we eat, and how our pussy smells *and* tastes will be directly affected by what we eat and drink. Eating fatty or fried foods and a diet filled with a lot of red meat will definitely have a negative impact on the way you taste and smell. Also, watch your alcohol consumption. Alcohol dehydrates the body, and when the body gets dehydrated, it tends to smell strong and taste stale.

DIRECTOR'S NOTE

Did you know that it's believed that men can actually subconsciously detect when a woman is in her fertile time of the month by picking up extremely subtle odors she emits? And these are the very odors we're told to douche away!

Some more simple advice: if you know you're going to be intimate with someone, be sure to bathe beforehand. Also, use a gentle soap that's not overly perfumed—men want to smell and taste *us*, not the perfume in our soap. After you bathe or shower, you will feel more confident and ready to wow him!

The "Inferior" Orgasm

In my quest to break through my own inhibitions I also became aware of another factor holding me back from asking for what I need: the idea that my way of having an orgasm was inferior. As outrageous and even silly as that may sound, when I had this revelation it felt so right that I knew I was on to something. Shere Hite reported in her last book (*The Hite Report: The National Study of Female Sexuality*) that a full 70 percent of women she interviewed did not achieve orgasm through intercourse, yet many still feel that they *should* be able to climax this way and that there is something wrong with them if they can't. While many women climax wonderfully through oral sex, my personal favorite is to manually stimulate my clitoris while my man stimulates my G-spot with his fingers.

Ever since my early days as a virginal eighteen-year-old when my boyfriend used to get me amazingly excited by finger fucking me, I've always loved the feeling, and it remains for me a great way to get off. I know this is a rather common favorite with many other women as well, particularly because it enables them to have their G-spot stimulated. Yet I realized that I felt awkward explaining this because I feared not only that perhaps the man wished I would get off by him fucking me or going down on me, but that my way of achieving orgasm was actually inferior. What with all the literature touting the new ways for women to come, it begins to feel like a performance. Years ago it was a great liberation to bring women's orgasms to the fore. Men were finally paying attention to the fact that we too were capable of climaxing and in fact *wanted* to climax. But now it's gotten to where if we don't we fear letting the *man* down.

Years ago Freud had the nerve to label the clitoral orgasm as "inferior." That misinformation has been put to rest, but now it is assumed that women are supposed to be driven to heights of ecstasy by oral sex or G-spot sex and we're even supposed to ejaculate! This isn't to say that many of us don't go wild from these delicious activities and have female ejaculations, but it seems that whenever new information comes out about our sexuality there sometimes comes along with it a sense of pressure to perform correctly. In this way, our orgasm is no longer ours. Instead, our orgasm becomes a sign that a man is indeed a great lover and that we are "normal" because we're having orgasms the "right" way. It was becoming clear about these associations that helped me break through my fear of explaining what I needed to get off.

Letting Go of Inhibitions: Private Fantasies and Desires We're Afraid to Reveal

The area of inhibitions that's a bit more tricky to deal with are those that are brought on by our private fantasies and sexual desires. One word that should be stricken from our vocabulary when it comes to sex is the word *normal*. Let me begin by saying that there is no such thing as "normal" or "abnormal" when it comes to personal sexual tastes. And yet the most commonly asked question when people go to a sex therapist or counselor is, "Am I normal?" As most psychotherapists will agree, anything is fine as long as three factors are present: 1) the sexual act is consensual; 2) a fantasy or sexual interest does not interfere with the intimacy of a relationship; and 3) no one gets hurt. But I know from personal experience that's easier said than done.

When I first sexually came of age, I discovered that my most common fantasies were of being forced to have sex with anonymous men. Having been a young college feminist I was horrified by these politically incorrect fantasies. (*Politically incorrect* are two more words that don't belong in the bedroom!) Women were supposed to take charge now, I had learned. How could I succumb to such negative thoughts? How could I betray my sisters? These fantasies of mine remained locked away in shame and fear of ever being discovered. Then I got married. And even though I adored my husband and found him very sexy and our lovemaking quite good, I found to my frustration that I needed to conjure up my shameful fantasies in order to climax. I felt that he should be enough to get me there, and I was afraid to explore my fantasies and find out whether we might actually enjoy acting them out—not literally, just pretend. Eventually, my fears became like bricks in a wall, a wall that grew higher and thicker every time I closed my eyes and secretly fantasized, leaving my husband on the other side, cut off from my most intimate and revealing self.

And then two things happened that helped me break through my shame and inhibitions. The first was that I went to counseling and eventually talked about all of these shameful feelings with my therapist. The second was that I became involved through my work as a film director with the community of sexuality therapists, counselors, and researchers, attending many workshops that addressed these issues. Through both of these experiences, I learned that there was nothing wrong with any sexual fantasy as long as it was consensual and it wasn't hurting anyone, including myself. I also learned that suppressing my true desires tended to only make them bigger in my mind, gaining more and more power and consuming my sexual thoughts. This is true for all of us. In other words, you can't force your fantasies away.

The whole purpose of fantasies is to play with thoughts and ideas that you would otherwise not indulge in. While my husband and I went on to have a mostly happy marriage for several years and still remain close, it wasn't until after we separated that I was ready for my dream lover. When he and I finally met and discovered our mutual passion for fantasy, we became so familiar with and accepting of each other's fantasies that we could practically talk each other off. We liked playing with the fantasy of bringing other people into our bed but would never dream of doing so. Sharing fantasies provided us with all the excitement of a forbidden scenario, while keeping us safe from the potentially destructive fallout of such a situation. This sharing also bonded us in an amazing way. When two people can be so honest, so trusting, and so open with each other about something as intimate as their personal sexuality, they create powerful spiritual energy between them—as if their very souls merge together.

So it's important to examine any fantasies that you may have, and any negative thoughts or feelings you experience in relation to your fantasies. If you feel like something is getting in the way of truly enjoying your partner or your sex life, then you need to take action. Perhaps you need to examine how you feel about your inner fantasy life and the desires you feel. If you identify feelings of shame and embarrassment it might be worth it to seek some counseling with someone you can talk to in confidence about this, someone who won't judge you. (I'll provide a source list at the end of this book that will include ways to find a good counselor in your area.)

Fear of Being Judged

Another great source of inhibition is the fear that what we need or want will turn off our lover or make him judge us. If he finds out you like it rough will he think you are sick? If you ask him to spank you, will he think you're kinky? Such thoughts cross many women's minds and become an issue for them. Sometimes these fears have more to do with our own discomfort with our particular needs. As mentioned above, it's important to examine our own feelings and judgments about our needs. If we're afraid to make our needs or fantasies known to our lovers it may very well be because we are the ones judging ourselves and projecting those fears and judgments onto our lovers. Once we become comfortable with who we are and what we like, we are less afraid that these desires will turn off someone else.

I know it's still difficult to share such personal needs with a new lover. I have found that such things often come up in a sort of organic way, like with my lover who lightly tapped my butt while having intercourse and discovered how wet it was making me. But if you're finding that your man is not going in the direction you'd like him to, one of the more subtle and less direct ways to ask for something is to refer to it in a movie or an erotic story or some other "third party" situation. For instance, if you're watching a steamy movie together, whether it's a triple X, a cable TV soft-core feature, or some hot Hollywood steamer, and the couple begins engaging in something you'd like to do, you can turn to him and say, "Hmmm, did you ever think of trying something like that?" He might surprise you by getting very excited that you're so willing to try something so adventurous and different. Most men are very happy to find a woman who wants to spice things up with new ideas and ways of making love, or fantasies to play out. The complaints I get most from men are that women aren't adventurous enough.

On the other hand, if he acts shocked or disinterested, perhaps you need to open up and honestly communicate your desires to him. Again, that takes your becoming comfortable enough with your own needs so that you're not ashamed of them and not fearful of what he thinks. We all need to remember that nothing in our personal sexual lives is dirty or bad or sick. We live in a culture that's still not comfortable with sex and tries to get us to conform with arbitrary standards of what's decent and correct. Remember, until quite recently it was still illegal to have anal sex in several states in the United States! If you're worried about your own sexual desires, search the Internet for support groups for your particular interests and listen to what others have to say. It's imperative that you become comfortable with yourself in order to ask for what you need and not fear judgment from your lover. And if that still doesn't get you what you want and you want to be with this man, then perhaps you have to just try and strike a compromise: one night you have sex his way and the next night you have sex your way. Most men are more than happy to accommodate their partners and are very happy when they find out what really gets them off.

One couple shared this story with me: after being together for almost six years, the woman, Carol, was becoming increasingly frustrated with her inability to share some of her fantasies with her husband. In general she said she was satisfied with their sexual relationship, but she really wanted her husband, David, to know about one special fantasy of hers. What was it? To have sex in a public place. Why had she kept this fantasy a secret for so many years? She was afraid David would think of her as an exhibitionist when it wasn't that she actually wanted to be seen but rather to do it in a forbidden place. But as is the case when most couples share their fantasies, David was not only happy to play out Carol's secret desire; he was totally turned on—even by the thought of it! They went on to make a wonderfully playful and sexy game of attending big parties and sneaking off to other rooms to make love.

And let's not forget that men are not immune to such fears either. Many a man has complained of his inability to get his woman to try new things and fears being labeled and judged by his more virtuous wife. It's ironic that so many men choose to marry an inexperienced "good" woman, and then complain bitterly of an unsatisfactory sex life because she's too inhibited to play and explore different ways of having sex with him. It's no wonder there's such a demand for prostitutes. Imagine going through life never being able to explore and experience the wonderful varied pleasures of sexual love that you know you're capable of. It might be enough to drive *you* into the arms of a stranger . . . and it *has* driven many women into the arms of a stranger.

A man I know shared with me that he very much liked being dominated by the woman he loves and that it was important to him that any woman he gets involved with be willing to do this with him. He eventually met and fell in love with a woman who was willing to take workshops on how to be a good dominatrix and found to her delight that she not only liked it but that it opened her up to a whole new layer of her own sexuality that she was previously unaware of.

Opening up to each other is what fosters intimacy and true bonding. If you can't be open with your lover, you need to examine your feelings and look into what's holding you back. Are your concerns valid? Is your partner really judgmental or is the fear of being judged based on something else?

Learning about ourselves and accepting ourselves are the first steps to becoming an inner sexual star. Don't let ignorance, lack of self-knowledge, or fear of reprisals get in the way of your sexual pleasure and the intimacy you could be sharing with someone. When it comes to being able to love and be loved, accepting yourself for who you are and your partner for who he is are crucial—both emotionally and physically. Ultimately this acceptance and knowledge makes us better lovers. If we know how to listen to and care for ourselves, we'll learn how to listen and care for others. Comfort, confidence, and self-acceptance are aphrodisiacs. They enable us to be nonjudgmental of both ourselves and our lovers, and they enable us to share the joys of pleasure and sexual play with those we love.

DIRECTOR'S NOTE

The only time a particular sexual need or fantasy or fetish can actually have a negative impact on a relationship is when it's so consuming that it actually gets in the way of real intimacy with your partner. A good example of this comes from one woman who wrote to me that the only way her new boyfriend seemed able to get off was by completely restraining her arms above her head, rendering her quite passive, and eventually straddling her face so that he could climax in her mouth. She found this quite unsatisfactory, as it left her feeling as though she wasn't an active participant, unable to touch or do things to him, not even give him a good blow job! She began to wonder if it was actually *her* who turned him on or if it could be any woman pinned below him. Worse, it seemed he really couldn't get to the point of climax any other way. This points to more of a compulsive sexual behavior and one that sometimes is a symptom of one's fear of intimacy. By being so in control and rendering his partner completely passive the man is able to deal with his fear of vulnerability in the face of love and sexual intimacy. If you find yourself in one of these types of situations you might try first speaking openly and candidly with him about how it makes you feel. While you don't want him to feel judged, you can point out that it's not allowing you to enjoy the sex as much as you could. You might be able to change the scenario bit by bit, so that eventually he can get off in a variety of ways. In this woman's case she might agree to be restrained for *part* of the time while he has intercourse with her to climax. Another time, she might perform oral sex on him while keeping her arms free to touch and caress him. In other words, you're trying and adding variations to his way of getting off while still including some of the components he needs. If this approach doesn't work, you might both need to visit a sexual counselor together. It's important that *both* of you are having your sexual needs met in order for a relationship to become intimate and mutually fulfilling.

DIRECTOR'S NOTE

Never use the following words for sex:

- ○ *Should.* You either like or dislike something. Something is either a turn-on or a turnoff. Sex is one of the few things in life where you get to do what you like. No shoulds or shouldn'ts! (Except maybe that you *should* be sensitive to your lover and his needs too!)
- ○ *Normal.* Nothing in sex should be measured as normal or abnormal. As long as it's consensual, compassionate, responsible, and no one's really getting hurt, there's no such thing as normal or abnormal sex. Sex is sex and it's grand if you're both happy and getting off!
- ○ *Politically incorrect.* Leave politics out of the bedroom. Life is tough enough! Sex is the only place where we get to play and let go and not be in control all the time. And that whole idea that mistakenly came out of certain factions of the feminist movement, that women should deny their fantasies of being taken and submitting to our lover's desires, is completely wrong.

Prepping for Preproduction

The following is a list of questions you might ask yourself during your personal research phase. By answering these questions openly and honestly, you can discover your innermost fantasies and uncover any potential roadblocks that might get in the way of your sexual potential.

1. Are you comfortable touching yourself in private?
2. Are you able to bring yourself to orgasm through self-pleasuring?
3. Are you familiar with your sexual anatomy and how your body becomes aroused?
4. Do you enjoy playing with sex-enhancing toys?
5. Are you comfortable with the way your body looks?
6. Are you confident your lover finds you sexually attractive?
7. Are you aware of any inhibitions, fears, or feelings of shame having to do with your sexual desires?
8. Are you willing to investigate the emotional underpinnings of such inhibitions?
9. Are you comfortable with your own desires and those of your lover?
10. Are you in touch with your fantasies?
11. Is there a particular fantasy that you have never shared with anyone?

In the next chapter, you will take your research notes and begin to shape them into your script. By becoming even more familiar with your fantasies and sexual desires you will get ready to play them out—in real time! Now go explore your inner sexual thoughts and fantasies. Think about what your perfect erotic scene would be. Once you've got those images going in your head (and maybe in your groin!) it's time to develop the story. Is it a sensuous indoor picnic with lots of tasting treats spread out through the course of a long lazy afternoon? Perhaps it's a dark nighttime story that begins in a smoky bar pretending the two of you don't know each other, and ending up in your own private dungeon that you've set up at home. Or maybe it's something as simple as greeting your man at the door wearing nothing but a baby doll and handing him his favorite aperitif.

Chapter 2

The Script

The only way to get rid of temptation is to yield to it.
—Oscar Wilde

The Movie Moves On

I n the research phase, you learned how to examine and collect information about your sexual self, making you more familiar with your own desires and fantasies. You will now feel better prepared to take the next step in your journey of discovering and exploring the key to your sexual pleasure. And just as in the making of a film, the next step is putting together your script. Of course, scripting your sexual fantasy doesn't necessarily require you to sit down and draft anything. Rather, it means putting into action what you have learned about yourself sexually and coming up with the intention and the plan to play out the scenario with your lover.

When I am producing and directing a film, once I've decided what I'd like to say about sex or what kind of sexual story I'd like to convey in my movie, it's time to develop the script. In a film, a script is the blueprint for what happens on screen. It includes not only the lines actors exchange and the development of a story line, but also the director's cues to the actors about the tone and goal of each scene.

One of my movies, *My Surrender*, is a perfect example of how you can plan out your own sexy scenario. It's about a woman who videotapes couples acting out their favorite fantasies for their own private use. In one scene we see a couple sitting together talking. The woman says she's always wanted to see what it felt like to be more in charge during sex and wants to play out the fantasy of being a lady pornographer who auditions hot men for her movie. Her husband isn't so sure about this idea, but goes along with his wife—to his ultimate satisfaction by the end of the scene. We see this hot couple play out the woman's fantasy, beginning with the image of the woman reclined on a sofa dressed in a business suit with a sexy bustier showing underneath and black stockings and heels, smoking a cigar and putting him through his paces. She instructs him to strip for her. Once he performs his striptease, she calls him over for a closer look at his goods. Eventually the sofa becomes the casting couch with him performing his best moves on her. Every time the husband thinks he's wowed his wife with his studliness, she ups the ante and makes him do more to impress her. The next thing she demands is that he perform oral sex on her. Like so many men who believe performing oral sex on a woman is sufficient foreplay and makes them a great lover, her husband thinks he's got the role now. "Not so quickly," she says. Then she makes him fuck her. "Not bad," she says dismissively. Egging him on, he gets fiercer and fiercer—all to her delicious delight. Finally, he asks her if she wants to see his come shot, which he deposits on her luscious breasts. This last request was my way of poking fun at the surprising number of men in my private life who have automatically assumed that would appeal to me because of what I do!

The key to both the fun and the sexual excitement of playing out this scene for the couple was that the woman actively played a role in making her fantasy come true; she wrote *and* directed the script. Again, creating a script does not require you to actually write anything. I'm not suggesting that you write a feature-length screenplay. But if you want to explore a particular fantasy or see what a certain sexual move feels like, then you need to help make it happen. One of the first things a filmmaker learns is that a good film is all about making sure you're adequately prepared. Just as well-planned preproduction is the ticket to a smooth film shoot, in order for sex to be wildly satisfying, it has to be planned—it doesn't magically happen. This is not to say that I don't believe in the hot rush of spontaneous sex. But what about the other 364 nights of the year? There's nothing more fun and satisfying than occasionally planning out an erotic, exotic, and completely out-of-the-ordinary sexual scenario!

In that same movie, *My Surrender,* another married couple loves the idea of playing the professor and the naughty schoolgirl. The filmmaker helps them set up their script by creating a set with such simple elements as a desk and a blackboard. The couple dress their parts: he in a rather professorial-looking suit and bow tie and prim glasses, she in a cute red-plaid pleated skirt and white knee socks and red shoes. They pretend that she's his student and has arrived at class unprepared, has been routinely misbehaving, and has turned in poor exams and reports. Naturally he must resort to teaching her a lesson and punishes her by having her write on the blackboard over and over, "Lisa Ann must not disturb Professor Sir in class." As she writes this, she catches her prim professor eyeing the pretty legs and ass that are peeking out from under her skirt. She becomes more flirtatious and teases him mercilessly until he realizes he must *really* teach her a lesson. At that point he bends her over his desk and administers "corporal punishment." Eventually the two become very excited, and, while still remaining in character, proceed to have hot and heavy sex, starting off with him making her perform oral sex on him.

This scene is particularly fun because the couple is an actual British married couple and their accents make the role playing seem even more authentic. While you certainly don't need to have a British accent to carry this fantasy off, the point here is that the viewer gets to watch a couple set up a common fantasy scenario. They created a script of sorts, a blueprint, that would give them ideas of what to do and say to each other. They knew she would be the bad girl who knows her nerdy professor likes her, and she teases and taunts him mercilessly, eventually driving him wild with desire so that he takes her right then and there. Is he *really* the one in control? That's for you to answer—and to play with.

Of course, in the films I direct, I include more than one scenario, more than one character, and sometimes more than one story line. A film would seem flat or boring without such varied dramatic elements. But when you are planning a sexy evening with your special someone, it's probably best to keep things simple, which is not to stay that you can't ditch your script and head in whatever direction suddenly appears. In fact, one of the most important things for a director to keep in mind is the ability to be flexible. One never knows when some disaster on the set will necessitate a change in script or character. For example, in *Three Daughters,* one of the actresses turned out to be so intimidated by working on this project that she took a mild sedative that rendered her unable to remember her lines. As a result I had to rewrite the scene at the last minute, giving another actress most of the lines.

This could happen in real life too. Perhaps your mate won't feel comfortable in his given role or maybe you both hit on something else that's even more exciting. It would be a good idea to remain sensitive to cues, such as whether your partner seems to be enjoying the scenario. If you get the sense that he is nervous or not into it, you might decide to veer off in another direction. For instance, some men might agree to being dominated but in actuality don't feel completely comfortable in that role. While they may be willing to give it a shot, you might sense a growing discomfort on their part and allow it to go in another direction. Nothing is much fun if both of you aren't enjoying it. Go ahead and create some guidelines, a blueprint of sorts to go by, and at the same time allow the scene to evolve on its own. Pay attention as a good director would. While I will script exact lines for my actors, if I sense they're not comfortable with saying them exactly as I've written them, I sometimes allow them to improvise. This allows them to bring something of themselves to the role and usually guarantees a far better and more convincing scene.

Creating Your Own Sexual Scenario

What fantasy have you wanted to play out for some time? Being taken and ravaged? Being the powerful woman in charge of your man? Do you want to don a costume and play dress-up for a night? Let's talk about some of the kinds of "scripts" you can come up with and how to prepare. I've found that there are several standard types of fantasies that women vary in their own unique way. Here is a list of the most common fantasies for women:

- To be forced, ravaged, or taken, the proverbial "rape fantasy"
- To have sex with someone other than their partner
- Idyllic encounters with an unknown man
- To dominate or be in charge, directing a man to give her sexual pleasure in whatever way she pleases
- To be an exhibitionist
- To have sex with more than one man
- To have sex with a woman
- To have sex with a famous movie star or rock star
- Watching others have sex

Scripts with a Hidden Message

I sometimes describe my Femme movies as "sexy movies with a hidden message." In other words, I'm scripting them with the intention of subtly inserting whatever sexual lesson I'm sharing. Sort of what sex coach Dr. Patti Britton and I call "edutainment." You too can drop a subtle hint to your lover by creating a scenario that will get him to try something your way. Let's say you, like many women, wish your lover would slow down and spend more time in that teasing, petting stage. Creating a scenario is often the best way to really get your point across. In one of my movies, *Bridal Shower*, we see a group of girlfriends celebrating together and exchanging gifts. One of the women brings a big basket of sex toys and movies as a gift. This gets them to talking about how they got their men to be the lovers they want. One woman talks about how she needed to get her man to slow down and be more sensual, so rather than simply try and instruct him, she came up with a way to show him dramatically, by playing it out. Then we see how their scene unfolds.

She plans a picnic for them in a lovely setting up in the mountains of Malibu, filling her picnic basket with all sorts of delectable fruits, pastries, whipped cream, and other goodies. She wears sexy white lace undergarments underneath her long flowing summer dress, topping off her outfit with a big straw hat. The couple heads off to the mountains to enact her secret little scene. Once there, she heads off his eager grabs with offerings of sensuous fruits to feed to each other. She gets him to sensuously taste the succulent fruits and rubs them along her body for him to lick off her skin; she spreads whipped cream on him and licks it off. Because she has secretly planned the scenario, she's been able to show him the fun and pleasure of taking time to taste and lick and savor. Without coming off like a teacher or a drill sergeant, she's engaged her man in the sensual pleasure that comes from slowing down and taking your time as opposed to rushing toward intercourse. This is one example of how you can script your own scenario that will teach your lover how to best please you. Here's another.

A friend of mine recently confessed to me that whenever she senses her husband is horny and wants to have sex, she starts to undress in front of him. But instead of letting him touch her once she is naked, she directs him to sit on the bed as she then dons her favorite lingerie. She then mounts him and begins to touch her own body, as she enjoys the pleasant sensations of his hardening penis underneath her.

As you create your own scenarios, be mindful of what messages you want to convey to your lover: Do you want him to be gentle or more rough? Faster or slower? Talk dirty or talk less? Once you determine what you expect from your actor, the better able you will be to direct him.

CANDIDA CLOSE-UP

Q: Does the average woman like a little foreplay or a lot?

A: We are all different, so the best thing is to ask your partner what she likes. Communication is essential for good sex. But if I had to generalize, I'd have to say that women tend to like a lot of foreplay. In fact, it's best to drop the word *foreplay*, which implies that real sex is intercourse and the rest is all just leading up to it. It's all sex, and the more creative the better. Do a lot of touching, kissing, oral sex, fingering, intercourse, back to oral sex, take a break, back to intercourse, maybe more oral sex or fingering—you get the idea. We tend to think that a bit of oral sex and then intercourse is all it takes, and then it's over. But there's so much more. It's best not to be so goal-oriented and just do what feels good when it feels good, and ask your partner what feels good to her! Sex researchers say that it takes women on average twenty minutes to get warmed up, so not only do we like a lot of foreplay, but we need it!

Getting Ready to Role

Part of the fun and excitement that comes with playing out your secret fantasy or desire is revealing it, and yet this unearthing of a long-held secret can be very intimidating. Our inner fantasies can be a very sensitive issue for us. Yet each time we close ourselves off—out of shame or embarrassment—we erect another brick in the wall between us and our lover. On the other hand, when two people can openly and honestly share this most intimate part of themselves it is incredibly bonding.

The more you try and repress a particular fantasy or desire, the stronger it becomes in your mind. You can't push away fantasies and desires. The best way to deal with fantasies is to find someone you love and trust with whom to play them out. In fact, this is the idea that inspired the scene in my movie *Three Daughters* between the oldest daughter and her beau when they playfully take turns restraining each other to the bed with scarves and stockings and then pleasuring each other.

In this scene the oldest daughter has been away working in London and has come home for the holidays. Her fiancé comes over and before announcing that he has found a way to follow her to London and live and work there, he playfully says he's "never going to let her go again" and ties her wrists to the bedpost with lingerie that's lying on the bed. In order to show that it's completely consensual and not really forced, I had him ask her, "Is this OK?" to which she playfully responds, "I like this!" Then he teases her with feathers and kisses and licks her until she has an explosive orgasm through oral sex. Then she tricks him into being tied up as well and teases him and pleasures him and drives him wild until she unties his wrists and they really go at it, bringing him to a fierce climax. All consensual, all playful, and all really hot.

During my own years of therapy I came to understand that the proverbial rape fantasy is for many women a way to give us permission to let go. Because so many of us still feel a sense of shame or guilt or fear of letting go enough to climax, imagining that we are being forced to give or receive pleasure enables us to turn the control switch off in our brain and actually let go enough to climax. What renders us unable or fearful of letting go varies in different women. In my case, as I disclosed in my introduction, it was being assaulted in the park at the age of thirteen. Even though I managed to fight this man off and escape before he could rape me, I still suffered the trauma and resulting impression that my blossoming sexuality was dangerous because it caused men to "lose control" and want to do bad things to me. As a result, I came to see the act of losing or giving up control as a dangerous thing and I found it difficult to let go enough to let someone bring me to orgasm. My "rape fantasies" provided me with an imaginary "on" and "off" switch. Once I closed my eyes and pretended my husband or my lover were forcing me to have sex, I was able to turn off the controls and let go enough to climax. This was probably also a way for me to act out something that really almost happened to me, but in my fantasies (or by playacting the scene, which I'll go into next) I got to actually be in control and thus heal the wound it left in me. One way I learned to not feel like I was betraying my husband was to imagine him as the person in my fantasy. But the best was when I was able to bring my lover completely *into* my fantasy. Not that I would imagine my lover as that horrible man in the park, but rather that *my lover* wanted me so badly that he was determined to take me in any way he could.

Giving in to my fantasies of surrender also liberated me. It empowered me enough to try being the dominatrix, and I discovered that there was a real powerful she-woman inside of me, something I never would have known had I not given myself permission to first give in to my longings to be the submissive woman. Similarly, if you have a fear of revealing a fantasy, consider therapy or counseling as a means by which to understand, face, and dispel your fear. Once you are empowered to reveal your fantasy with your lover, you'll be better able to script a scenario to make your fantasy come true at last.

Some women's process of letting go and giving themselves permission to indulge their fantasy is less complicated and less difficult. But they have to take conscious steps nonetheless. In the case of one woman who wrote to me via my Web site, her secret fantasy was to be tied up. She discovered through reading my Web site that this was very common—lots of women were into a little B&D (bondage and discipline). With a sense of both relief and excitement, she planned her evening. She purchased some soft silk scarves especially for the occasion, adorned her bedroom with candles, and then wrote a note to her lover: "Would you be so kind as to use these scarves to subdue and ravage me?" The results were extremely rewarding and opened up a whole new level of passion between them.

Directing Your Man to Deliver Your Fantasy

I was married for nine mostly happy years to a lovely man who remains like family to me, but, like many couples, we eventually grew in different directions. Because we had never had children to be concerned with, we agreed it might be better for both of us to move on and discover what else was in store for us. I realize this flies in the face of the sanctity of matrimony, but I don't believe every single relationship or marriage is meant to go on forever, nor that divorce is always a failure but rather something to learn from for the next great love in your life.

I also had felt for some time that having come to terms with my personal fantasies, there were sexual dimensions I longed to explore that I wouldn't be able to if I stayed in my marriage. My husband, who was moving onto a more spiritual path, didn't share my particular sexual interests and, being a self-described pleasure baby, I couldn't bear the thought of not exploring my sexual potential. There was a whole world of sensual exploration and fantasy play that was burning inside of me and ready to be unleashed.

After we separated I had the good fortune of meeting and getting involved with a tall, dark, exotically handsome man who shared my steamy fantasies and longed to play and go in that direction as well. How did we come to realize this? First of all, I'm convinced we are able to read clues about people that we're not even consciously aware of. I was fascinated with this man for some time before actually going out with him. He was the assistant conductor of a jazz chorus I had joined. I would watch him quietly stand before the chorus until we all realized he was waiting for us to quiet down so he could start the rehearsals. Was it his subtle way of controlling the group without having to say anything, or the stern look on his face as he stood there waiting for us to notice and fall into line? I don't know. All I do know is that when it finally became evident to me, once we actually began dating a couple of months later, that he was my perfect passion match, I marveled at the fact that I had managed to find the exact man I could finally live out my fantasies with after coming to accept them in myself—the latter probably needing to be firmly in place before being open to finding Mr. Right.

How did we discover we shared the same fantasies? It certainly wasn't that we sat down and quizzed each other about such personal matters. Finding out what your new partner likes can be a tricky business that usually requires paying attention to subtle cues and clues more than coming out and asking. If you're able to ask your potential new mate what he likes right off the bat, more power to you. That is as long as your new man is not intimidated by your sexual frankness and is able to be honest about such things before knowing you very well. I have found that this sort of discovery phase happens in a more organic way between lovers and that finding out that you and your new paramour are sexually compatible is actually what helps in creating the glue that begins to turn you from you and him into a "we." For my new man and me, our compatibility wasn't completely evident at first. In fact, because he spent so much time being slow and sensual for the first several dates, which I adored, I began to wonder if I had made a mistake. But when I began to fantasize about him dominating me, I knew I had stumbled upon my first clue that this sexual match was going to work. I have found over the years that when you can put a new lover into a certain role in your fantasies, it's usually a good indication that he probably shares those leanings himself. Again, it's that intuitive sense that we're not even necessarily conscious of. But after such a long, drawn-out period of soft sensuality, I began to think he was more the tantric lover than the fierce dominator I was looking for. (Though, as he certainly showed me, the best doms are those that are also sensitive and sensual. And indeed, this man was the most sensuous lover I had ever come across up to that point in my adult life.) All that changed after one session of lovemaking where I was on top with my back to him. He began to very lightly and gingerly pat my behind and noticed pretty quickly that it was making me very wet. He was noticing the clues!

We later finished our lovemaking by laying down and masturbating together—something that I think is great partner play. It allows you both to observe how the other likes to be touched and get off. Afterward he asked me what I had been fantasizing about. At first I was shocked. No lover had *ever* asked me to be so candid about my inner fantasies. I didn't even know if I could answer him honestly. I was afraid, like many women, that my lover would think I was weird or sick. But then I began to consider that I hadn't done all that work in therapy for nothing. I took a deep breath and told him the three fantasies that had been playing in my head, all of them having something to do with being taken, maybe even by more than one man. To my relief, this seemed to really turn him on. However, when I then asked him what *he* had been fantasizing about, to my dismay, he was unable to tell me. While feeling a bit frustrated that I had disclosed to him what to me was so personal, I decided to leave it alone.

When we got together next time he apologized for chickening out and finally admitted that he had been completely amazed because he had been having two of the same exact fantasies as I was having. We realized that we had been fortunate enough to have each found someone with whom we could finally explore a rich and fertile playground that had been living unattended in our minds and longing desperately to come out and play.

So what enabled us to know? We paid attention to the clues we were giving each other, and we were able to open up and talk about what was turning us on and what we were fantasizing about during sex. Being able to be so forthright definitely requires a certain level of comfort with our own sexuality. But I hope that once you've been through your own research phase (as discussed in chapter 1), you will gradually become more comfortable with this degree of openness. You also have to feel a sense of trust and comfort with the other person. You can be sure I would not have been so open with someone I had just begun to date. This man and I had been together about two months before this scene unfolded for us, and it was clear we genuinely liked each other and saw the other as a potential long-term mate.

I cannot express how liberating and fulfilling it was to find a man who delighted in the same kinds of fantasies as I had. But it's also wonderful when you find a man who can also be creative and set up provocative scenarios for you both to play. I recall one evening arriving at his house to find he had elaborately set up an erotic set—just for me. He called it our "black-and-blue" night, and had set out nothing but black and blue scarves with which to tie me up. Then he darkened the room, leaving only candlelight and just a couple of blue lights on. All I had to do was go and change into the sexy black lingerie he had bought for me to wear. And the music? While you might have guessed the blues, that would have been too easy. This man was far more exotic than that and played a selection of Gregorian chants for us!

As you may have guessed, the black-and-blue theme was also a double entendre for the fact that he took great pleasure in spanking me. Of course he never actually left black-and-blue marks—as any experienced spanker knows not to do. Needless to say, the care he took in assembling such a well-thought-out and erotic environment for our long, luscious evening really set the tone and induced in me a feeling of great desire and anticipation. I actually learned from him how wonderful it is to take such care in preparing every detail for an erotic evening with your lover and how special it makes a lover feel. I can assure you, I took his lead and prepared many a wonderful evening for him as well.

How to Choose Your Leading Man

When casting the leading men for my movies and planning out the erotic scenes, I try as best I can to replicate what I feel is the perfect lover. I'm not always successful, since I'm dealing with real men who have their own ideas and ways of making love, and short of jumping into the scene and doing it myself, my direction can only go so far in getting them to touch and make love to my actresses the way I'd like them to. But every so often I succeed in portraying the kind of sex I see as ideal and the kind of lover I myself would love to find. And how do I find this perfect leading man?

This is a question I get asked a lot. People often hope I'll have some juicy and titillating casting couch tales. But as cute and hunky as some of my auditioning studs might be, I don't believe in mixing business with pleasure, so I must find creative ways to get a glimpse of what kind of on-screen lover these men would be.

First, I spend some time casually talking with them about themselves, the project, the goals of Femme Productions, and what I'm trying to portray through my work. This step gives me an opportunity to see if they get the concept of my work and the idea of erotica from a woman's point of view. How these men talk about themselves often reveals how they like to make love. I recall one actor calling me up and boasting, "I've got ten inches and I can get you lots of girls for your movies." I knew immediately that he wasn't right. Any man who thinks size is the most important qualification for being a leading man is missing the point. I also disliked the pimp mentality implied in his statement.

What I look for in leading men are statements of how much they love to please women and how wonderful it would be to have the opportunity to actually make love to a woman on film rather than just perform the acrobatics evident in so many standard porn films. If a man wants to be a lover of women as opposed to a stunt cock, I know he may be a perfect leading man.

Another qualifying factor for a leading man is that he be a lover of sensuality and that he make love in fluid, sensuous ways. However, these criteria are not easy to detect from an audition. But one technique I've used involves having an actor and an actress audition together. Once they've read lines together I ask them to go behind a screen or some other area created for privacy and ask them to undress and then come out. Once they're in front of me and I get a look at their bodies and whether they're in shape and without grotesquely huge tattoos, scars, or piercings, I ask them to lightly caress each other—no genital or blatantly sexual touching, just a gentle embrace and a bit of caressing. This enables me to see how they use their hands. Does the man caress the woman sensuously or does he touch her in a matter-of-fact, perfunctory way? Does he seem to enjoy touching her or is he more into impressing me with his studliness? (The men aren't the only ones I'm concerned with. I like my actresses to be sensuous lovers as well.)

And if I don't have an actress with whom he can audition, I ask him to caress himself, his arms and chest, to get a sense of how he touches, for we tend to touch ourselves the way we touch others and how we like to be touched ourselves. Though not perfect, these little tests do at least give me some basic idea of how a man feels about and interacts with women.

However, when it comes to casting your own leading man, it's not always so easy. We can't sit and interview the guy nor can we ask him to undress and caress himself in front of us, so it becomes essential that we pay attention to subtle—and sometimes *not* so subtle—clues. The first thing you need to know is what kind of leading man you're looking for, in terms of both his personality and the type of lover he is. Do you want a high-energy guy with a high libido who likes to grab you at the most unexpected time and place and have a robust quickie? Or do you like someone who's more calm and laid back, who likes to linger over your body and make love for hours on end? Once you know the kind of lover you want, it's important to learn how to identify the character traits as well as the physical signs that go along with that particular kind of lover. Perhaps you're like me and know exactly the type of man you prefer as a lover. I always look for a man who I think is going to be a very sensuous lover and who is also highly passionate and creative. I call myself a slow burn, someone who begins the day slowly and calmly but who can then work for many hours straight, without a nap or a break, and who ultimately can stay up very late working or playing far into the night.

I have the same style when I make love. I adore beginning with soft caresses, burying my face in my lover's silky skin and caressing him all over as he caresses me. This gets me very excited as we work ourselves into a froth of intensity until we're ravaging each other for hours. I also like a man who's interested in knowing what pleases me, who takes joy in finding fun new creative ways to make love and exploring new terrain.

Once you have a mental idea of what you're looking for, then you need to gather some clues to see if the man you've chosen fits the bill. First I'd pay attention to how he acts with you over a romantic dinner date. While I always think it's a good idea to be a good listener and to be interested in getting to know a lot about a potential new man, you also want to feel he's curious about you and what you have to say. I've been with many men who are so intent on impressing me that they regale me with stories about themselves and never once get around to asking me anything about myself, which may be a hint of what's to come in the future. Also watch out for the guy who asks you something and when you begin answering, you notice his eyes wandering around the room checking out who else is there. Not exactly a turn-on, and a good indication that this may not be a man who's going to be sensitive to who you are and what your needs might be. All women need a man who seems genuinely interested in who you are and what you have to say, and it is this kind of man who is more likely to be a lover who will take pleasure in finding out what you like in bed and how to give it to you.

You may also want to watch the way a man eats. This advice often amuses people, but I find it's almost always a good clue as to what kind of lover he'll make. It's pretty easy to figure out. Does he scarf down his meal as if he can't wait to get to the next activity? Or does he take his time savoring each bite and enjoying each unique flavor? I recall the first time I tried out this test. My date ordered ice cream for dessert. I watched as he slowly slid a spoonful of ice cream into his mouth and pulled it out with some still remaining, and then sensuously slid the spoon back into his mouth and finished it. I thought, *I think I've lucked out.* Sure enough, this man became the lover who would introduce me to lovemaking that was sensuous, passionate, and creative beyond my wildest dreams. Just as with his ice cream, he made love to me slowly, sensuously, and for hours on end.

Now, I'm sure you're thinking, *Come on, Candida, how can you tell all that by the way a man eats ice cream?* Well, obviously it wasn't only the ice cream, but it was, shall we say, the icing on the cake. It was the way he sensuously enjoyed his food combined with the way he looked at me with a sizzling passion in his eyes. It was how interested in me he was and how wonderfully he listened when I spoke. It was his willingness to share stories about himself and the depth with which he spoke of things, showing a desire to probe more deeply rather than skim the surface of things. It was the quiet confidence he displayed rather than the loud bravado of men who are more interested in parading themselves like a peacock. Such men do not make good lovers or partners; they're far too interested in themselves to know or even care how to make a woman truly happy.

The most important idea to keep in mind when you are trying to select your leading man is that one facet of a person's personality is often indicative of how he is in all facets of his personality. The same holds true, of course, for women too. For example, if you are a creative person in how you approach your work, you're probably creative in the way you approach most things in life, including making love. If you meet a guy who's a multitasker, who grows bored easily and needs to move on to new things all the time, beware, he just might be that way in matters of love and sex too. If you want a sensitive lover who's genuinely interested in you, look for a man who's kind and sensitive in general. Does he open the door for you and let you enter first? I know in these days of female independence we're not supposed to want such demonstrations of chivalry, but as a longtime feminist myself, I've learned that in our culture these are signs of courtesy and respect that show you a lot about how a man was brought up and whether he was taught to respect women and treat them well. And watch the way he treats others. Sometimes a man will shower us with special favors to impress us and then treat the waiter with disdain and condescension. Beware of such selective behavior: once he thinks he has you, he might not be so nice to you either.

If you want a man who is sensuous, pay attention to how he touches you when you're out on a date. Does he put his arm gently on your back when helping you into the car? Does he hold your hand when you're walking and does he do it gently? Or does he grab it and hold it as if he's tugging at a jammed door? When we began dating I noticed that the man I'm with now adored massaging my shoulders and back. A real good indication that this man liked to touch and caress, and boy was I right!

It's all about paying attention to subtle clues. Does he seem attentive and sensitive to you? Does he treat you with respect? Does he like to hear what you have to say? Does he touch you sensuously, even just to help you on with your coat or help you into a car? Does he meet your gaze when you speak? Does he use his hands nicely and take his time enjoying his meal with you?

Pay attention to these things. Men will let you know exactly what kind of partner they'll be right from the get-go—*if* you're paying attention. If it's just a fleeting affair or a hot one-night stand you're seeking, then don't worry about it. But if it's a leading man you want to keep in your life, pay close attention to how he treats you, how he treats those around him, and yes, watch how he eats his dessert!

Beware the Red Flags

When you *are* casting for a potential lifelong partner, beware of the "red flags." First, let me say that I don't consider every relationship that doesn't turn into an eternal lifelong commitment to be a failure. Sometimes, as with my nine-year marriage, people stay together for as long as is good for them. I know this attitude may fly in the face of our conventional definition of matrimony, but in these times when we can expect to live well in to our eighties and maybe even older, someone we choose to be with at twenty or thirty may not be the same person we want to be with many years later. He may change, we may change, and our needs may change. I felt that my marriage was perfect for me during that time. There were no red flags to look back on; we simply grew in different directions and wanted different things for ourselves and from our primary relationship.

That said, there *have* been relationships that I felt were mistakes because there were signs right at the beginning that should have made me stop and not proceed. But I ignored these red flags and I paid for it in the end. At a certain point in my adult life, I had suffered from no less than three of these mistakes in a row. I looked at all three relationships and searched for patterns to see if there was something I needed to watch out for in terms of my own behavior or choices. What I saw was that in every case there were very clear signs of potential problems with each of these men that I went on to ignore or believe I could change. To better illustrate what I mean, I'll describe each one:

The first guy I just adored. He was passionate and sweet and kind and intriguing, but he was dirt poor and I knew deep inside that unless he made some drastic personality changes, I would not ultimately be able to spend my life with him. Now some of you may be saying, Well, why not just have an affair with him, why do I have to commit "for life"? It's not always that easy. We were falling in love and we both knew this was no brief affair. Because I was so drawn to him I decided to try and overlook his financial state. Didn't I work hard to become a liberated woman who could take care of myself and not choose a man for his money? But eventually the culture we live in begins to poke its nose into even the most liberated relationships. It wasn't just me who wished he could afford to take a vacation but it became *he* who resented the fact that I would pay both our fares in order for us to take a trip. And finally when the subject of marriage came up, I was forced to

confront the reality of what life would be like with him and realized it wasn't what I wanted. Ultimately I had to walk away, breaking our hearts in the process.

The guy after him was sexy and fun and had a promising career
but at a certain point early on I realized his looks and charm
masked a self-absorption that rendered him insensitive and sometimes even obnoxious. I confronted him about this but he was so
smooth in his response: "I love a woman who doesn't let me get
away with stuff. Help me work on this." I fell for him—and his response—hook, line, and sinker. Needless to say he *never* "worked"
on anything, and I had to get out of there after two long years of
ultimately feeling drained and overshadowed.

The last guy was amazingly charming and sexy and fun, but
showed early signs of being a sexual withholder. He'd come on real
strong sexually one day and the next show a cold lack of interest in
making love or even being affectionate. He too had the right answer:
"Help me work on it." Eventually, while declaring his eternal love
for me, he showed less and less sexual interest. I found myself eventually feeling insecure about my desirability and confused about
what he actually felt for me. I finally had to extricate myself from
this two-year relationship when I was just too unhappy to go on.

These last two "mistakes" are good examples of how we women
often think we can change a man and set out to do so. Men often
feed right into this challenge by volunteering to make themselves
our project and then get angry when we indeed try to change
them. The bottom line is that I ignored my own warning voice that
said this man is not right for me.

Here's what you need to know in order to recognize and listen
to your red flags when you see them:

1. You'd better like who the person is when you meet him, flaws
   and all. No one changes, not for you, not for love, not for anything. Occasionally we do work on ourselves and if *we* want to

change ourselves, we might do it. But don't count on it. Basically, no one can change another person, and most of us can't change ourselves, no matter how hard we try. So like him, or leave him now.

2. Watch out for the red flags. If you feel something doesn't feel right, pay attention. Does he have a personality trait or a character flaw that you truly don't believe you can live with? Listen to your instincts; they are your best judge. We can really talk ourselves in or out of things, but our gut feelings always can be trusted. Don't ignore the trouble signs, and most of all, don't convince yourself you can change them. And I don't mean little things that you can live with; I mean big: he's unable to earn a living or live in the style you want to live in; he's incredibly self-absorbed; he runs hot and cold and makes you feel insecure about yourself; he shows abusive or violent tendencies. If there are things you can't live with or he makes you feel bad about yourself, leave. He's not going to change.

Life is too short and at a certain point we come to realize that we don't want to waste time on the wrong person when the right person could be out there waiting in the wings. My good friend Veronica Vera once said to me that relationships shouldn't have to be such hard work. Sometimes we're lucky enough to get it right and things just go smoothly. Yes, a little work is sometimes in order. Now when I see that red flag glaring in my face, I force myself to walk away before I get in too deep. That's what dating is for: to find out whether it can work or whether there are warning signs or red flags to heed. It's better to enjoy a brief fling and a small disappointment than a long mistake and a broken heart.

The bottom line is that you should be with someone who makes you feel good about yourself. I learned to ask myself one very basic question when I became confused or conflicted about whether or not I should stay, and that question is, "Am I happy?"

This may sound overly simple, but it's one that gets right to the heart of the matter and can be very difficult to answer truthfully when you don't want to know the truth. I answered truthfully when it was painful to know the truth.

YOUR ROLE AS LEADING LADY

Having the kind of sex you want also depends on what kind of lover *you* are. It's not just up to the man to be sensitive and sensual and creative and fierce. It's also up to the woman. Nothing turns a man on more than seeing his woman writhe in pleasure and excitement at his hands. Just as we like to feel beautiful and desired, the man likes to feel like he's your perfect lover and the one you absolutely want. And it's not just about responding to him; it's also about taking initiative and sweeping *him* away. Men like to be caressed and swept away into heights of ecstasy just like we do. So when we identify what we can expect from a man, we are also describing what he should expect from us. It's no longer acceptable for women to lie back and passively be pleasured. A woman who can also take a man to places he's never gone is a woman whose man will cherish and keep her happy. I always like to say, the way to a man's heart is *not* through his stomach, it's through a place just a little farther down!

Creating His Fantasy

Being a great lover is about both giving pleasure and receiving pleasure, so your script one night may be to give *him* his favorite fantasy. If you happen to know that he has a particular fantasy or sexual activity he's longed to play out, what better gift than to give him that opportunity? As I mentioned before, giving myself permission to surrender and submit to this loving and accepting man with whom I got to act out my fantasies (and with whom I had a long passionate relationship with for a number of years) enabled me to switch roles as well. It turned out that he too wanted to find out what it was like to be dominated and to surrender to someone. While at first I didn't know if I could really pull off such a role, how could I not accommodate this man who had so wonderfully helped me live out my long dormant and desired fantasies? So I looked at some photos and scenes of women dominating men and watched what they did and how they acted. Then I selected the proper attire and created a scenario or a script I could act out in. I learned too that a good dominatrix isn't necessarily mean or cruel, but rather gently in control. Many men love the idea of giving up control because of how our culture requires them to always be the one in charge. In a way there's nowhere else but in the bedroom where we can truly give up control and have it be OK.

So I became the woman in charge, strutting about in my black garters and stockings and sharp high heels, taunting him by turning him on but refusing to let him touch me until I let him. I instructed him to pleasure me in any way I wanted to be pleasured, and if he didn't do it right he would be slapped and maybe even hit with my riding crop! It was only if I instructed him that he'd get to fondle my breasts or lick my pussy or lick and caress my feet. Eventually I would allow him to mount me; but it was only when I was fully satisfied that I would allow him to come, and even then, I would choose how he got off.

It turned out to be really fun and quite liberating to see how in charge of sex I could actually be. And I truly believe it was only because I had liberated the part of me that longed to be taken that enabled me to switch sides. In fact, the truth about most professional dominatrixes is that many of them start out as submissives and actually still prefer to be taken by a strong man in private. By the way, that was something he explained to me as well—that it was far more fun for him to sexually dominate a woman who was, like me, quite in control in her everyday life, strong and in command. As he put it, it's no fun to sexually dominate a woman who's already submissive in her daily life. The thrill is in turning a powerful woman into one who melts at your every touch and does everything you tell her to.

I want to point out here that this kind of sex play is not something we did all the time. It's important to feel that you and your lover can also have regular ordinary vanilla sex as well (a term used to describe sex without any sort of domination or kinky play). The only time you know a particular sexual proclivity might be unhealthy is when it's the *only* way you or both of you can get off. Like if your man can't get inspired to make love to you unless you dress in black leather and whip him, you may have a problem there. It could mean he's a bit obsessed, which might get in the way of any real intimacy. Besides, it's important for us to feel that our lover wants *us* with or without the fantasy. And this man always made me feel it was me he wanted and not the fantasy I was occasionally playing for him. He would sometimes spend long periods of time lovingly caressing my body and I his before making plain and simple love. In fact, what I came to discover was that by getting to live out this long-hidden fantasy of mine so thoroughly with someone I loved and trusted, this particular fantasy eventually lost its grip on me. It was no longer this powerful longing in me, and eventually faded into being just another game in my sexual bag of tricks that I could take out and play with when I wanted.

This is why counselors will so often talk about the importance of facing and exploring such sexual needs rather than trying to repress them. As I said earlier, you can't repress such powerful needs, they won't go away; they'll just get stronger and stronger until they sometimes even become an obsession. But if you can find someone you trust enough with whom to safely act them out, they'll more than likely lose their grip on you and, as with me, become something you occasionally like to do.

D I R E C T O R ' S   N O T E

An important word of caution here: trust is a major key element in being able to open up and share your fantasies, especially those involving any sort of force or domination. You need to feel comfortable with the person, you need to *trust* the person, and you need to be mindful of how he might react. If you're into playing the kind of fantasies I described, whether it's the mild control and surrender or more intense physical pain, it must be done in absolute consent and safety. You might want to read up on such sexual play or watch an instructional video. I will give additional suggestions in my resource list, but keep these in mind:

○ *Never* play such games with a stranger or someone you don't know very well.

○ *Never* allow yourself to be restrained unless it's with someone you know and thoroughly trust. Most people who are really into this lifestyle will tell you that they actually have safety words or phrases that let the dominant one know they don't want any more or it's gone too far, and they'll also tell you that it's really the submissive person who's in control.

○ *Never* play with something you don't fully understand.

Not every fantasy is this extreme. There are others that may be more tantric, more spiritual. This can be a wonderful way for lovers to learn the more sensual art of love and help teach men to slow down considerably, taking the emphasis off of his orgasm. I will also list books and videos and places you can take wonderful workshops together in my source list.

More Fantasies to Play

There are more traditional games to play, like the "happy hooker," or "Mrs. Robinson and her boy toy," or the exotic dancer. When I began seeing the man I'm with now, I knew he had been fond of going to strip clubs and getting lap dances. Some women might feel threatened by knowing their man likes doing that, feeling like they have to compete with these anonymous women. I instead decided to become his dream lap dancer and provide a private show for his birthday. Since we were going away for the weekend, I was limited to having to do it in a hotel room, but that didn't stop me from planning out every detail of what I would wear and what music I would dance to. Most modern hotels now provide small stereo systems complete with CD player. All I had to do was bring my favorite CDs. And I didn't even have to worry about creating ambient lighting—the hotel's lights were on dimmers, allowing me to still create a soft, sensual ambience for my performance. Even without this added convenience, I could just as easily have taken a silky scarf or piece of lingerie and draped it over a lamp to soften the lighting or give the room a little color.

How did my man react? Needless to say he was completely blown away, especially when I had him teach me what the lap dancers actually do. So not only did he get his favorite kind of sexy entertainment from his favorite woman, he also got to live out the fantasy of taking it all the way to the bed. And I can tell you I was duly rewarded. Now he knows the best place to come for a fabulous striptease and a lap dance. And, rather than feeling threatened by his penchant for such sexy play, I look forward to providing him with such private entertainment again and again.

Many men love to have their woman striptease for them. Some women recoil from the idea of striptease dancing, thinking that it is objectifying or cheap to perform for a man in such a way. I've always thought of striptease as an art form, or another type of dance. I've always loved the idea of enticing a man and driving him wild with desire. I also think it makes a man feel really wonderful to have you go out of your way to create something just for him. If your man is someone who's been fascinated with this sort of thing, there's no better gift you can give him than to become his own private dancer. And you don't have to do it like everyone else does. Sure, you can go and take a course in stripteasing; they'll show you all the typical moves and ways to gracefully remove your clothes without getting caught in them and feeling foolish and clumsy. Then you can go on to create your own signature dance, one that combines what he likes with who you are as a woman and a goddess.

Fortunately, I had studied various types of dance for many years, and was always fascinated by the art of erotic dance. When I was fifteen, one of my best friends' mothers, who was a very sexy Puerto Rican woman, put on a 33 RPM record featuring Little Eva, a striptease dancer from the sixties. My friend's mother then proceeded to show us how to dance sexily for your man. I was mesmerized! I had seen the movie about the legendary Gypsy Rose Lee when I was fairly young and found her absolutely fascinating, with her mix of intelligence, her proper behavior, and her ability to tease men into a frenzy without ever getting completely naked. I liked that she mixed class with sexiness. (In fact Gypsy's signature dance evolved from her mother's pushing her into striptease dancing, despite her lack of confidence or feeling pretty or sexy.)

I have always preferred Gypsy Rose's more subtle classy approach to striptease to the more cliched bump-and-grind style used by strippers of yesteryear. When I began doing what we called personal appearances as a porn star in the late seventies, early eighties, where a theater would show one of my movies and then I'd come out dancing and stripping, I put my knowledge of erotic dance to use and combined it with my years of classical dance training and jazz singing and came up with what I called "Isadora Duncan meets Gypsy Rose Lee." I prerecorded music to sing campy old standards like "My Heart Belongs to Daddy" and "Whatever Lola Wants," moving on to more contemporary music to which I would slowly and enticingly strip. This became my signature erotic striptease. While my career as an erotic dancer was a bit short-lived due to the rather seedy environment of many of the clubs and theaters, I loved when I'd find myself involved with a man who enjoyed this sort of play and I took great pleasure in setting up private shows for him.

You too can find your signature dance based on the kind of music you like, the sort of dancing you like to do, and how you see yourself. Are you a subtle tease or do you like the idea of putting on pasties and strutting your stuff like a real strumpet? And what does your man like? When packing and planning my private little show for my new beau, I asked him what kind of lingerie he likes: the traditional garters and stockings look? Or a more contemporary look that might involve thong panties and thigh-highs? He liked that I was putting so much thought into the event and his anticipation grew. I then selected music that turns me on and inspires me to dance in sexy ways. Music is a great transformer. Let it come through you. The more you just feel the music and respond to it, like you do when a good lover is touching you in ways you like, the less you'll have to think about *what* to do. Do you find yourself swaying to the R&B rhythms of Marvin Gaye or do more contemporary sounds get you in the mood? The hypnotic tones of South Asian and Middle Eastern music mixed with the great dance rhythms of world beat or hip-hop really put me in the mood. It's important to find music, lingerie, and a style of dance that suits and inspires you. (You will find music suggestions in chapter 4 and lingerie suggestions in chapter 6.) It's not enough to do something only to please someone else. The more you actually feel it the more it will show and the more of a turn-on it will be.

What is your man's fantasy? As with women, men have some standard fantasies that they then make unique. Some fantasies, like being with two women, might not be something you want to actually act out. One must be very careful when it comes to opening up your relationship to others. There can be unexpected fallout that can damage the all-important trust that bonds you. I have known of couples who are able to successfully bring in others, but for most of us this is not an option. What *is* an option, however, is playing with the fantasy of it together. But again, it requires absolute trust and confidence that *you* are the one he wants and *he* is the one *you* want. One woman told me that her husband loved the fantasy of being with her and another woman. Because she was not comfortable having a real ménage à trois, but was willing and interested in playing out her husband's fantasy, they compromised by reading some erotica that featured three-way sex with two women and a man. "I never thought I would get so aroused, but the whole scenario got me so hot!" she reported. Their being able to compromise in such a safe yet creative way led to many a hot night for this couple.

One of my lovers loved the idea of watching me with other men but would flip out if it ever really happened. We were able to play with the idea in our fantasies and scenarios because I made it very clear to him that while I too enjoyed that fantasy, I in no way wanted to be with anyone but him. I also happened to like the idea of being forced to watch him with another woman. Because he made me so confident that he wanted only me, I too was able to play with that forbidden fantasy in our role-playing.

POPULAR MALE FANTASIES

If you're not sure what your man's fantasies are, try these prompts, and remember, it doesn't mean you have to actually *do* these things. It might mean *pretending* to do these things:

- Being serviced by a private masseuse
- Being with two women
- Sex in a strange place (the ladies' room at a fancy restaurant, a stairwell in a hotel, etc.)
- Sex with strangers
- Being forced and told what to do
- Being served by a high-class call girl

Soon you will take your fantasy—and maybe his—one step further toward reality when I show you how best to prep your set. You will learn how to use lighting, furnish your love nest, and add music so that your fantasy can come alive in 3-D! But first, let's turn to the masters for more inspiration.

Chapter 3

Studying the Masters

To sail the entire length of a body
Is to circle the world
—Giocanda Belli, *Brief Lessons in Eroticism I*

Any good director uses her script as a kind of blueprint for her film, letting it focus her on the goal of the picture. At the same time, it's just as important to turn to the masters of your genre for inspiration and advice. In this chapter, you will see how watching erotic videos and porn films can not only give you sensational ideas for your own script, but when you share them with your lover and watch them together, you can find a hot, highly charged way to enjoy each other sexually. I've also included other ways to enhance your lovemaking skills with erotic stories, pillow books, and other sources of sexy words.

X-Rated Movies: To View or Not to View

The topic of viewing erotic or pornographic films can be a touchy one for many women. We've grown up in a culture that drums it into us that good girls just don't go for that sort of thing. And it's not difficult to buy into that stereotype considering all the bad porn that's out there. Let's face it, most of it has catered to some of men's most base fantasies, devoid of any real attempt to show what women actually like. I've often said that if men *really* think women reach the height of ecstasy by having come spurted in their face it's no wonder they've got to get their rocks off by watching porn!

But the truth is that women in fact *are* turned on by the visual. If we weren't we wouldn't be oogling pictures of Brad Pitt and Johnny Depp and I'd be out of business! There have been a number of studies that were conducted to test out whether women really *do* or *don't* respond to erotic imagery. Women were put into a dark room by themselves and outfitted with tiny receptors hooked up to their vaginas to measure their physical response, and then shown a variety of sexy images. What the researchers found was that most women would say that they were *not* turned on while in fact those little receptors belied them! In other words, they *were* responding physically, but because of years of indoctrination and being told that women are not visual, they fooled even themselves. They simply couldn't admit it to themselves or anyone else how turned on they were by the erotic or pornographic images.

A study that went even further in exploring this actually used a scene from one of my movies, *Urban Heat,* and was published in the "Week in Review" section of the August 13, 1995, issue of *The New York Times.* It was a scene in which a forty-something woman seduces a twenty-something elevator operator in a commercial building. Women have always liked this scene because of how reinforcing it is to see an average-looking woman, not a "perfect blond with an impossibly beautiful body," to quote Dr. Ellen Laan, who did this research, and who, even at forty-something, is in great shape and obviously confident and comfortable with her body as well as her sexuality. The character is completely in charge and really puts this young man through his paces, making sure she gets what she wants! It's also not particularly explicit, yet it is incredibly hot and highly charged. This woman is clearly enjoying herself and there's no question that she is indeed having not one but two or three orgasms during the scene.

Dr. Laan, a professor at the University of Amsterdam, conducted this study to see how women responded to women's erotica versus typical male porn. The results were very interesting. While the women seemed to physically respond to both, their subjective responses were markedly different. According to Dr. Laan, "They reported positive emotions and sexual arousal about the woman-made film, but quite the opposite about the man-made film," which was apparently fairly crude and mechanical. She further explained that, "Our subjects were telling us they were aroused by a film when they liked the film. The sexual arousal they reported was due mostly to how they appreciated the situation." In other words, even though they registered a physical response to both, their dislike of the content and ultimate discomfort with the male scene made it impossible for them to enjoy it, while the more female-centered scene gave them permission and made them feel OK about what they were seeing, thus enabling them to register and acknowledge and *feel* their pleasure. This result proved that while women are indeed turned on by visual stimuli, it's important for them to like and feel comfortable with the content in order to be able to truly enjoy what they're seeing.

I never in any way want to make women feel like they *must* enjoy watching porn or erotica. There are way too many other things to do in the arena of sex to feel pressured into something we don't like. On the other hand, I also feel like it's a woman's *right* to explore and enjoy porn and erotica if she is so inclined. It's important to watch erotic movies not because your lover is pressuring you, but because you:

o enjoy watching sexy movies yourself
o are curious to find something you yourself like
o are honestly *willing* to give it a try because your lover would like you to

The other important thing is to find what you or both of you like. There's nothing worse than finally deciding you'll try something out only to end up with the absolute worst garbage that turns you off to the idea forever. There are lots of different kinds of porn and erotica out there, what with over ten thousand releases a year now, most of which unfortunately are trash. So how do we sift through it all and find what we like? A few pointers:

1. Listen to the suggestions of women-friendly erotic stores, catalogs, and Web sites (listed in the resources section), and purchase the videos through them.
2. Go by the director. A distributor can sell all levels of product from the low-budget gonzos and amateurs to the high-budget, soft-focus erotica, but a director will always leave her stamp. There's no confusing a Candida Royalle movie with a Seymour Butts movie! With each one you *know* what you're going to get.
3. *Don't go by the cover.* Some companies spend almost more on their cover photography than they do on the movie inside.

CANDIDA CLOSE-UP

Q: It is my theory that men are more visual when it comes to sex, and that women are more auditory. Do you know of any sexual audiotapes for women? I strongly feel that there is a whole unexplored territory in terms of women's sexual fantasies; I think you have helped in this regard but there is still so much to be untapped, or unleashed!

A: I know that Lisa Palac had done a CD of audio sounds, and there may be more. But honestly, I don't think they're really such big business because otherwise there'd be many more. This tells me that women aren't all *that* thrilled with audio only. Women are visually stimulated but by subtly different imagery than men. They don't want just eye candy; they want to see the lovers really connecting on more levels than just physical. They want to sense real passion and desire, real seduction and surrender to the moment. The long-term success of my Femme line tells me women are indeed visual. They just want it done differently than is customarily done for men.

Working Titles

Here is a list of different kinds of porn and erotica and directors you might consider. Remember, don't censor yourself. If you like down and dirty, go for down and dirty! Don't feel ashamed. Like I said, nothing is bad or dirty or abnormal as long as you're both enjoying it and no one's getting hurt. (And of course it's not kiddy porn.) And if you prefer softer or more story-driven erotica, don't feel like you have to show how nasty you are. Just the fact that you're willing to give it a go shows a willingness to break through outmoded taboos and explore new sexual dimensions.

○ Classics: This refers to big-budget adult features from the seventies and eighties. Women tend to like them because they often have good story lines, and the women are far more varied and real looking rather than what I call the Barbie-doll look. Many Web sites, like gamelink.com, offer these now due to their growing popularity. Look for directors like Anthony Spinelli, Henri Pachard, Chuck Vincent, Robert McCallum, Radley Metzger (who directed the famous *The Opening of Misty Beethoven*), and Gerard Damiano, who's famous for the groundbreaking *Deep Throat,* but whose *Devil in Miss Jones* is considered one of his best. Summer Brown's *Every Woman Has a Fantasy* was also a favorite for a long time.

○ Bob Chin: For a bit of silly fun, the work of director Bob Chin can bring some laughs. He produced and directed the *Johnny Wadd* series starring the infamous John Holmes with his unbelievable thirteen-inch cock. (And it *was* that big; I should know. I worked with him in my acting days. Whew! That was something every gal should get to try at least once in her lifetime.)

○ Andrew Blake: Many women really like his work because of its high production values, beautiful people, sets, and costumes. I find the sex still a bit formulaic and you should know there's an overabundance of "girl-girl" action, which puts some female viewers off. But he is quite popular with women.

○ Cameron Grant: I adore his very first movie, the original *Dinner Party*, which featured gorgeous people and very erotic scenes. It's also where I discovered Mark Davis, whom I used in several of my movies and is a real favorite with women.

○ Michael Ninn: Extremely high production values, strong plotlines that sometimes are rather bizarre, but be forewarned that the sex can be somewhat extreme at times.

○ VCA's Veronica Hart series: Veronica Hart is one of several former adult stars who stepped behind the camera to create some of the better movies on the market now. Hers are more woman-sensitive than much of what's out there, with strong plotlines featuring strong women, but she makes no bones about the fact that she likes her sex hard and explicit. Her *Edge Play*, starring Marilyn Chambers, received rave reviews from New York City's female-friendly emporium, Toys in Babeland.

○ Adam & Eve's Ultimate line: These movies are what I would call a "kinder, gentler" kind of porn, featuring dreamy stories and very pretty people. However, they too are still quite explicit and scenes often end in the obligatory facial come-shots.

○ Vivid Video: Known for high production values and strong plotlines, the work of former adult star Paul Thomas has garnered many awards, especially *Bobby Sox*. But these films are pretty explicit, and again, full of the almighty "money shot."

○ Shane's World: I can't vouch for this myself, but I know women who really like this sort of "gonzo for girls." Shane and her girl-friends are really in charge and clearly having a real fun time of it with the guys lucky enough to get invited in on the action. Explicit and heavy on "money shots," meaning exterior come-shots.

○ Nina Hartley's "How-To" videos: These are a great combination of Nina's wealth of knowledge as a "sex educator" (a self-proclaimed feminist who graduated magna cum laude in nurs-ing) and fun hot sex with her "friends" as they act out what she's just "taught" them. Not big-budget extravaganzas, but in-timate and hot nonetheless.

○ Candida Royalle's Femme line: I would be remiss were I not to mention that my films are very popular with women due to their woman-friendly approach: story lines with real characters and issues, what I call sensuously explicit erotic depiction mi-nus those overused money shots (you'll never see a facial come-shot in a Candida Royalle Femme movie!), light on genital close-ups, and the use of more "natural" women and often real-life couples.

What If He Wants to Watch Porn, but You're Uncomfortable with the Idea?

Don't ever feel like you must do something you don't want to. However, it's always good to be open and at least give something a try. You might want to ask yourself exactly why you don't want to watch X-rated movies with him:

○ Were you brought up in a strict religious household that looked down on such activities?
○ Are you worried that he may prefer the women on-screen?
○ Are you turned off to what you've already seen?

The last reason is easy enough to deal with: become an active part of the selection process. Research what movies are available, visit women-friendly stores or Web sites, order a catalog from one of the woman-friendly mail-order companies, and select those that other women endorse. Don't just rely on him to do the choosing if you've already been unsatisfied with what he's brought home. If you fear he'll prefer the women on screen to you, I'll refer to what my friend Dr. Marty Klein always says about that: it's not that men are generally looking at the women on the screen and wishing their woman looked like that; in fact many men find the overabundance of makeup and silicone to be quite a turn-off. If they're wishing anything, it's that their woman was as *comfortable* with her body and her sexuality as the women on-screen. I would add that it's what the couples on-screen are *doing* that's such a turn-on rather than what they look like.

My female-friendly Femme movies were recently the subject of an academic paper called "Reflexivity in the Pornographic Films of Candida Royalle," by two professors, James K. Beggan of the University of Louisville, and Scott T. Allison, University of Richmond, and published in *Sexualities*. They point out, "Another explanation for women's possibly lesser enjoyment of sexually explicit media concerns is that women tend to compare themselves to women in sexually explicit material. Because most women fall short of such ideals, looking at these media images may adversely affect self-image." They later go on to show how I address these concerns through the characters in my movie *Bridal Shower*.

Nina Hartley plays a married woman, Penny, who echoes these concerns by confessing to her friends that she feels threatened by the perfect women who appear in porn films. Her friend Claire (played by Missy) makes the distinction between a man being turned on by a woman and by what the woman is doing, that is, acting out a liberal sexual identity. Claire states that she stopped being jealous of women in porn films when she realized that men were less interested in those women in particular than in being involved with sexually open women. The authors go on to explain that the "exchange fosters a nonthreatening and positive reconceptualization of sexually explicit material: any woman possesses the potential to be as attractive as a porn star if she is willing to explore and elaborate her own sexuality." I couldn't have put it better myself!

I always tell men, if you really want your woman to watch a sexy video with you, you'd be well advised to make her think that in your eyes she is the sexiest woman alive. I'll share a personal story to illustrate that point. I had a lover some years ago who was delighted to discover that I had porn videos around my house. I actually wasn't even much of a watcher myself, considering that I find much commercially available porn boring and formulaic, but people often send me samples of their work for me to view. When he asked if we could watch some together, I said, "Sure, why not?" Because this man made me feel like I was the hottest and sexiest woman ever for him, I didn't feel threatened by the idea. In fact I used to pass on to him my girlie magazines that publishers would sometimes send me. (There was an unexpected benefit to watching X-rated movies with him as well. To my surprise I found that I even liked some of the raunchier stuff, and by being open to it, got in touch with some of my racier fantasies!)

Fast forward to a couple of years later when I was involved with the man who turned out to be a sexual withholder, making me feel insecure about my desirability in his eyes. To my dismay, I found that I absolutely could not enjoy watching X-rated movies with him. But it should have come as no surprise: without feeling confident that he desired *me*, how could I feel comfortable with him watching and enjoying *other* beautiful women?

So if you're feeling insecure about being confronted with images of other beautiful sexy women while viewing a sexy movie with your man, you might ask yourself the following questions: Does he make you feel desired? Is it you who is insecure even though he does desire you? And finally, are you able and willing to accept that he's not looking for you to be as perfectly beautiful as the women on screen, and that he's in fact *with* the woman he wants to be with?

If a strict religious upbringing is holding you back, it's important that you talk about it with your partner or husband and let him know. Remember, there's nothing wrong or bad that two people do together within the context of a loving, committed relationship. You may need to look at your personal issues if they are holding you back from sharing something that might otherwise be good, healthy, sexy fun between you and your man, as long as he's not asking you to do anything terribly unreasonable or suggesting movies that are so reprehensible that even the most liberal of us would be horrified. Perhaps talking with a counselor would help you sort through your feelings. And remember, you have many options. Most quality adult films actually come in two versions, sometimes even three versions. Triple X means very hot with lots of close-ups and money shots. Double X, or sometimes single X, means that they're still explicit but they don't have as many close-ups and they eliminate the "money shots." These are often referred to as "couples" porn, but some of what people call "for couples" can still be very explicit and full of come-shots; as I suggested, choose according to the director. Soft X, or nonrated, are sometimes referred to as "cable versions" because they are created for cable TV. These films are not explicit and definitely do not have the almighty "money shot." I welcome the challenge of editing my movies into nonexplicit versions. I sometimes even prefer them and feel it shows that you don't always need to be explicit to be sexy and stimulating. While many companies don't advertise these softer cable versions, you can certainly ask whether they are available. They may be a terrific way to break the ice and experience the joys of sharing erotic imagery with someone you love.

What If He Doesn't Want to Watch Porn and You Do?

I would say the same applies as if you're the one who's uncomfortable. No one ever said that women cornered the market on insecurity! Not to mention the all-consuming performance anxiety men often suffer from. Imagine this poor guy having to watch not only some of the most buff guys with what appear to be the biggest cocks known to mankind, but they're also seeing a guy pump away endlessly, able to hold back for as long as he wants while the hot babe on the end of that pole is screaming in ecstasy! All right, maybe some of the guys aren't that great looking, but standards are getting much higher now that women are becoming a significant part of the viewing audience, and there's a lot more pressure on guys these days to keep themselves buff as women achieve more economic independence and no longer have to stay in unsatisfying relationships just to make sure their rent is paid. You would do well to assure your guy that it's *him* you want in bed with you and that it takes a lot more than a big ol' shlong to keep you happy, and obviously your guy's got the secret or you wouldn't be there with him. Then you can go ahead and try to get him to learn a few things now that you've got him feeling like Tarzan, king of the jungle. But more on that later.

If *he's* got reservations due to religious beliefs, then I would suggest the same as if it were you. Talk about it, assure him that you understand and are not judging him, and perhaps even talk with a counselor if it's that important to you.

Remember, it's all for the good of your relationship to experiment with things like toys and movies, and it's important to let your lover know that *that's* your reason for wanting to do so, not because there's anything lacking. Simply explain that watching videos could be a fun addition to your otherwise *fantastic* love life.

What If You Both Want to Watch Different Kinds of X-rated Movies?

Maybe he wants something nasty and you want something softer and more romantic. Or, breaking those annoying gender stereotypes, you want to watch Seymour Butts and he wants to watch a gauzy, soft-focused bodice ripper on film. It's simple: take turns! And don't do it begrudgingly. Unless it's something that you find over-the-top objectionable, try and give a little—you never know, like I discovered about myself, maybe there's a nasty bitch living in you that you never knew existed. Once we cast off those old mores and stereotypes, we sometimes uncover a bawdy gal in there capable of more fun than we ever imagined.

Another suggestion I often make to women is to view some adult videos alone before watching them with your man. This will let you know what you like and don't like without having to worry about whether he prefers the actress on screen or any of the other nagging thoughts that sometimes go through our heads while watching with a lover. This might also show you that it's indeed what the lovers are *doing* rather than what they *look* like that's a turn-on.

BENEFITS AND USES OF WATCHING EROTIC VIDEOS WITH YOUR PARTNER

1. As a prelude to sexual activity or to jump-start the mood after a long day of work for the two-career couple (and being a full-time mom and housekeeper is a career in itself).
2. To add diversity to a monogamous relationship. Now that couples more than ever want to stay together as well as maintain a satisfying sexual relationship, rather than stray outside of the marriage, watching other couples can provide a sense of adventure and also offer examples of other ways to make love.
3. To enhance sexual desire. Sometimes people have low libidos

because it's difficult for them get in touch with their fantasies or perhaps they haven't formulated any yet. Watching adult movies can help them get in touch with their inner fantasy life. Sometimes it's also easier to recall a visual memory from a video that turned you on rather than a fantasy.

4. To open up a discussion of likes and needs. It can be very difficult asking for what we need, and sometimes being able to refer to another couple on-screen rather than referring directly to ourselves makes it easier for us to open up that discussion. For example, one partner can ask if the other ever thought of doing what the couple on-screen is doing, or they can suggest that they try having sex like the couple on-screen. Watching other couples on-screen can also model for the viewing couples how to assert oneself and ask for what they need.

5. Sometimes watching a particular kind of video, for example, one that shows a man being dominated, can provide a compromise when two people want different things. It can also show the other partner how to play that role for the other.

6. To provide suggestions and examples for expanding one's sexual repertoire. This can be helpful for people who are a little shy, and also for people as they age and perhaps need more stimulus to become aroused.

SITUATIONS WHERE ADULT VIDEOS ARE NOT SUGGESTED

1. Men with problems of premature ejaculation.

2. Some men with erectile disorder who may become even more discouraged watching others who function with relative ease.

3. People with a history of sexual abuse who may respond negatively to erotic videos, particularly aggressive porn where women sometimes appear to be degraded or objectified.

4. People with poor body image. Perhaps amateur videos, featuring average people with less than beautiful bodies, would be a better alternative to the more studio produced adult erotica.

Words and Pictures

Another way to find inspiration for your own love story is to get inspired with words and pictures. I'm a big fan of reading erotic stories for ideas to jump-start my inner fantasy life, so why not share the experience with your lover? Take turns reading sexy sonnets to each other, or dabble in hot erotic fiction. Or take a stab at writing your own erotic stories and scenarios. Perhaps you could act them out afterward. It could be a great way to find out what ideas *really* lurk in the mind of your lover. Erotic stories can be an incredible aphrodisiac, especially when they reflect your own fantasies. I had one lover who could practically talk me off by guiding me through imaginary scenarios taken right from my own inner fantasy life. He was amazing at it; it was a skill he acquired by being a voracious reader of erotic fiction himself.

And what about pictures? Erotic imagery has long been acknowledged for its ability to inspire. In fourteenth-century Japan a Japanese noblewoman created the first pillow book. In Japan, pillow books have long been a traditional gift exchanged between lovers. They take their name from the lacquered wooden "pillows" of Japan in which these conveniently small works of erotic instruction and amusement were usually kept. Erotic gift books have been enjoyed by lovers in China and India from the very earliest times. Nowadays we have all sorts of sexy coffee table books and those too racy to leave out in the living room to choose from. A visit to your local bookstore can provide countless possibilities, from the highly stylized work of Helmut Newton to the more down-to-earth *Erotic by Nature* collection of writings and photos edited by David Steinberg.

You might even feel inspired to try photographing your honey in the buff, or let him photograph you. Or go to a professional photographer to create sexy boudoir photos of yourself for your guy.

EROTIC STORIES AND OTHER WRITINGS

o Anne Rice's *Sleeping Beauty* series is still very popular.

o Susie Bright has a great collection of erotic short story books, with her most recent Tenth Anniversary Edition of *The Best American Erotica 2003* getting rave reviews.

o *Sweet Life: Erotic Fantasies for Couples*, edited by Violet Blue.

o *Best Women's Erotica*, edited by Marcy Sheiner.

o Nancy Friday made waves over twenty-five years ago when she published *My Secret Garden*. A collection of real women's fantasies sent in to her, this myth-shattering book burst through the misconception that women do *not* have fantasies! A new updated version was recently released.

HOT MAINSTREAM MOVIES

If you're not into the triple-X genre of adult movies, there are a growing number of movies that cater to women's fantasies and sensibilities like my Femme line of films—"erotica from a woman's point of view." Or you can check out the growing number of edutainment videos that feature real lovers while teaching better love skills, like those offered by the Sinclair Intimacy Institute. For a more spiritual or tantric approach, visit www.tantra.com. (See the resources section at the back of the book for more suggestions.) Of course, with Hollywood getting racier and racier, you don't even have to look at an explicit movie to see some sexually inspiring scenes. Some of my all-time favorites have been:

o *Body Heat*, with Kathleen Turner and William Hurt.

o *The Hunger*, with David Bowie and Susan Sarandon.

o *The Piano*, with Harvey Keitel and Holly Hunter.

o *Last Tango in Paris*, with Marlon Brando and Maria Schneider.

o *Bull Durham*, which kicked off the long-running affair between Susan Sarandon and Tim Robbins.

o *9 1/2 weeks* is still a popular R-rated favorite.

Phase Two

Preproduction

Chapter 4

Music and Lighting

I always say the difference between pornography and
erotica is in the lighting.
—Gloria Leonard

Let There Be Light

Have you ever seen those cheap, overlit porno flicks where the
scenes are flooded with light, making the actors' skin look
pasty and bringing out every unfortunate blemish on their
skin and butt? Revealing such detail should convince you of the
importance of lighting in any erotic situation. If you want to make
your skin look creamy smooth, if you want your body to glisten
and glow as you make love, then you need to pay attention to the
kind of light you use.

When I set out to shoot a scene in a film, the one aspect of prepping a set that takes the longest is setting the lights. You *must* provide ample lighting to make sure the image comes out on film. But
good, subtle lighting is also a crucial way to bring out the best in my
actors and set an erotic mood. In the old days (as in the *Boogie
Nights* era) when we used to shoot more on film, lighting had to be
substantial due to the delicate nature and technical requirements of

film. In the past, because budgets for adult movies were not as ample as Hollywood production budgets, they didn't have the time to spend on more creative lighting that would have been more subtle while still producing sufficient light. As a result, in order to counteract the glare of harsh lighting and all the imperfections it illuminates on one's skin, we gals used to apply pancake makeup to our entire bodies to give it the creamy glow of flawless skin. There we were, all the actresses, helping each other cover every inch of our skin. That alone could have made for quite a sexy scene! Needless to say it was a lot of work and the makeup often ended up on the sheets and furniture by the end of the scene.

Nowadays, many of the better adult film directors tend to spend a lot more time playing with lighting, and the actresses no longer have to cover themselves in messy makeup. While some cheapo productions still pay little attention to lighting, I make it an essential part of any scene—it's absolutely key to making a scene come alive in a sexy, beautiful, erotic way.

Lighting is just as important to the scenes we create in our own bedrooms or wherever we're setting out to make love. In fact, I take great pains to always have soft, flattering light in my home. After all, not only do I simply appreciate a warm inviting ambience anytime and anywhere in my home, I also want to be ready for that special time I choose to be with my lover. A sexy encounter doesn't always begin right in the bedroom, but often starts out in the living room or even the dining room. Sure, I have the practical lamp for curling up next to my cat to read a book. But when I have other things on my mind, my living room is aglow with a variety of soft lights strategically placed around the room to evoke a feeling of warmth and comfort. For me, overhead lights are a painful glare reserved only for cleaning and searching for a lost item that might have rolled under the couch.

Setting the Lights

So what sort of lighting do I prefer? I stock up on bulbs that range from soft pink to warm amber. My favorites are those that are called Indoor Color Reflector 50-watt bulbs that come in various shades of amber. I place these in lamps and directionals in order to cast a lovely glow around the room. I also have a small lamp with a red glass-beaded shade that creates an interesting pattern on the wall. Long ago I learned from a couple of very artistic gay roommates (gay eye for the straight *girl*) how to place lights behind plants and furniture to cast a colored glow from behind. Indirect lighting is far more flattering than direct or overhead lighting. Again, you won't be able to curl up with a good book under one of these lamps, but there's nothing like posing yourself seductively in the glow of this type of mood lighting—especially if it's strategically placed around the room to create a soft, warm, rosy ambience.

Rosy pink and golden amber lighting is wonderful for all skin types. Bright white lights have a blue haze, which highlights the skin's imperfections, such as veins and blemishes, as well as any redness or purple under the eyes from tiredness. Pink and amber neutralize the blues and redness of blemishes and tired eyes, instead giving the skin a warm, soft, creamy look. Women of color also fare much better under warm, soft lighting and should lean more toward the warm golden amber hues. None of us is perfect, but there *are* ways we can look close to it.

Of course, candlelight is also a wonderful choice for creating a romantic and evocative mood. The more candles the better. Just be careful with them; we want fire in our loins, not in our homes! And watch where you place candles in terms of how you want the light flickering on your skin. I've noticed that even when I place one candle in a candlestick, I can create a sharp shadow on my face and body. While most twenty-five-year-old women can't look bad, no matter what the lighting, the older we get the more our life experiences show up on our faces and bodies. There are simply more opportunities to create lines and shadows where we least want them. I've learned to move the candle away from my bed so that the lighting is soft rather than harshly reflecting on my face.

But keep in mind, if your man is totally into you and the passion you're sharing, I'm *sure* he's not noticing or focusing on the laugh lines on your face or the stretch marks on your breasts. After all, we're much harder on ourselves than our men are. But we want to feel confident that we look our best, so a little extra time spent on such details will ensure that we're focusing more on the good feelings we're experiencing than on whether we look OK.

DIRECTOR'S NOTE

I don't know about you, but the morning after can seem a bit cruel in terms of bright sunlight streaming across our bodies, highlighting all our flaws, not to mention the makeup we didn't get to remove before falling asleep in our lover's arms. If this is a concern for you, the obvious thing would be to have your curtains drawn so you're not woken up by this unforgiving light. But if you're like me, you love the morning sunlight and the thought of leaving the curtains or blinds drawn and shutting it out seems antithetical to beginning a wonderful fresh new day. I also happen to love morning sex and find it the most wonderful way to start my day. My solution is to have soft lace or pastel-colored drapes over my window so that the morning light is let in, but softly, so that it's caressing my skin rather than holding a flashlight on it. Hence, an erotic set rather than a cheap porno set.

The Set: From Basic to Boudoir in Minutes

And what about our set? Aside from the importance of lighting, which can actually camouflage not only the flaws on our skin but also a rather stark, unimaginative room, there are things you can do to make even the most boring room seem like a love den or a lioness's lair. First you must decide where you'd like your seduction to begin and where you'd like it to end up. If it's a first date or the beginning of a new romance, you might want to make sure your living room is conducive to seduction. We've already discussed the importance of having ambient lighting in place—whether it's an elaborate set of lamps, spotlights filled with soft warm amber bulbs, or strategically placed candles. But what about your furniture? Is your couch comfortable enough to sit on together as you draw closer and closer to each other? Is the fabric soft to the touch rather than rough and itchy to the skin? Do you have pillows that can prop you up should things begin to happen right there? Do you have small tables on which you can place drinks and luscious food items you can share and feed each other? Furnishings such as a comfortable sofa or big chair and adequate table space are basic items to anyone's living space, but with your script in mind, they can become magical props that ensure your evening of sweet seduction.

One of the easiest ways to spruce up a plain and uninviting room is the use of fabrics. Whether you go for exotic silks and satins or solids or prints, an attractive chenille throw or a piece of shimmering Indian silk can transform a boring piece of furniture into an exotic centerpiece. Add a few silk- or velvet-covered pillows to your couch, soften the lights, or light the candles and your functional living room can be transformed into an exotic Arabian tent.

The same goes for your bedroom. Whether you have a boring room containing no more than a bed and a dresser, or a princess room with frilly coverlets and your old rag dolls sitting on the bed, soften the lights, light a few candles, throw a silky fabric over the bed, and voilà! You've got a room ready for seduction! If you want to really get elaborate, try hanging a piece of silk netting or other filmy fabric over the bed. Years ago when I had my first very own apartment in San Francisco, all I could afford was a nice-sized studio. Being a single woman, I didn't want the dates I brought home to see a big bed as soon as they entered my apartment. Sure, it may have been the era of so-called free love, but I still liked the idea of a little seduction before retiring to the bed. So I found a way to enclose a small area by hanging room dividers around my double bed. Then I found a large silk parachute at an army-navy store and dyed it a warm peach color and hung it from my ceiling around the bed. The parachute fell beautifully all around the bed, draping the area in folds of soft, peach-colored silk. There was also enough room for a beautiful antique vanity dresser on which I placed a small lamp with one of my soft amber lights. I elevated the bed on crates hidden by my bedding so that it was more like a huge throne, and covered it with a softly colored bedspread, with a beautiful crimson velvet throw on top. Then I layered it with a large rose-colored silk pillow and several smaller pillows.

That first bedroom was perhaps the most inviting and erotic sleeping area I've ever created. In fact, I recall a friend of mine coming over for the first time and entering this erotic little area and declaring that she felt like she was in a big warm enveloping vagina. Can you imagine how my men must have felt? And all it took was a large military-issued parachute, some peach-colored dye, a hammer and a few nails . . . and a little imagination.

Don't be afraid to be playful. My friend the infamous porn star Vanessa Del Rio just loves her leopard prints and has no shortage of them in her private lair. Why, she even has a special breed of cat called a Bengal that has leopard-type markings to match! (A Bengal is a cross between an Asian Leopard and a domestic cat.) But better check whether your man has allergies before you go that far.

The Right Soundtrack

The other important element to a seductive scene or setting is the all-important music track. I've already talked a bit about selecting the right music that inspires you to dance and strip for your man. But what about music just for background? Because I'm the daughter of a professional jazz musician and have been a professional singer myself, music plays a big part in my life and in my work. I grew up in a household where music was always playing—whether it was the soft, melodic sounds of jazz or finger-snapping tracks of Frank Sinatra and Tony Bennett. I've carried on that tradition, finding music a warm and soothing backdrop that fills in the empty spaces as I go about my day working, reading, doing household chores, and especially making love.

When I set out to produce my first Femme movie, I knew that music would play an important role in creating an erotic mood. In fact, our early concept for Femme was the idea of creating erotic rock videos for women and couples. It was the mid-eighties and rock videos were all the rage. Plus it was a way for us to highlight what my original partner, Lauren, and I felt were the most important aspects of the genre we were creating: beautiful erotic visuals and good original music to go along. The added bonus was that we could eliminate the bad acting prevalent in most adult movies. If viewers didn't like our choice in music they could simply turn down the sound and play their own.

While we very much enjoyed the original music we had composed by a variety of musicians, we began hearing from some viewers who didn't share our penchant for what was occasionally hard-driving rock music. This made me more aware of how important our choice in music was to enhance an erotic mood. We also realized that music can sometimes be too dominating for a scene. People still wanted to hear the sounds of the lovemaking and complained when the music overpowered the natural sounds of the lovers. Eventually I chose to soften and play down the music in order to enhance the scene rather than dominate it. After all, we weren't trying to get people to get up and dance, we were trying to inspire them to make love!

The same holds true for the music you choose as a backdrop for your lovemaking at home. Music has a subliminal effect on us. It has the ability to transform us and take us places, just like good sex. You might want to think twice about putting on that throbbing techno dance music if you want to hear the sweet nothings your lover's whispering in your ear. Music should also have the kind of rhythm that matches the pace of lovemaking. The music should be as sensual as the sex you're hoping to have. One of the first pieces that comes to mind when people think of music to make love by is inevitably Marvin Gaye's wonderful recording "Sexual Healing." It's smoky, it's got a syrupy sweet rhythm to it, and the words are sexy as all hell. I'm sure there's no question as to what he had in mind when he recorded that!

For me what's important in a piece of sexy music meant to inspire lovemaking is music that's enhancing rather than intrusive, music with a sense of soft, warm rhythms, voices that are smoky and not grating to the ears, melodies that are exotic, and lyrics, if any, that are evocative rather than trite. Of course these qualities can reflect a wide variety of music for different people. My tastes tend to run toward the progressive; right now, I like the new South Asian music coming out of India and London that combines the exotic sounds of the East with world beat rhythms coming out of the West. For many, the smoky sounds of mellow jazz and R&B put them in a sensual mood. And for others, the sultry sounds of Brazilian music or the playful beats of the Caribbean take them where they want to go. Still others prefer a soulful ballad or a passionate aria as a backdrop to a sexual encounter. Sometimes the lyrics express what they are unable to. Whatever your choice, choose a piece of music that inspires you, that you like to move to, and that encourages your body to sway and undulate. Listen for rhythms that you and your lover can move to together.

Because of my love for dance, I often like to begin a seductive evening by dancing with my lover. Many men feel uncomfortable dancing and believe they don't know how. I have learned that if you have sultry rhythmic music playing that's easy to sway to, almost any man can learn to dance. All you have to do is get close and press your body up against his and slowly begin to sway to the rhythms. Eventually the swaying becomes an erotic embrace, the embrace turns into a kiss, and before you know it your hands are wandering, your tongues are exploring, and suddenly you are lost in the moment.

CANDIDA'S MUSIC LIST

I thought I'd come up with a few CDs to suggest, but after going through my collection *and* polling my friends, the list has grown! I include the label where possible.

JAZZ AND JAZZ BALLADS

Frank Sinatra (of course!): *Songs for Swingin' Lovers*—Capitol
Sinatra's Sinatra, with Nelson Riddle—Reprise
Nat King Cole and his trio: *The Complete After Midnight Sessions*—Capitol
Billie Holiday: *Lady in Satin*—Capitol
Charlie Parker: *Jazz 'Round Midnight*—Verve
Miles Davis: *Kind of Blue*—Columbia
Chet Baker: *My Funny Valentine*—Pacific Jazz
Diana Krall: *The Look of Love*—Verve
Etta James: *Matriarch of the Blues*—Private Music
My friend Gloria Leonard, a true jazz lover, suggests anything by Anita O'Day, June Christie, Sarah Vaughan, Billie Holiday, and Nancy Wilson, which I would have to agree with, as well as Dexter Gordon, Charlie Parker, Lester Young, Stan Getz, Al Cohn, Zoot Sims, Otis Redding, Ray Charles, and Gerry Mulligan.

R&B AND POP BALLADS

Marvin Gaye: *Love Deluxe* (with the aforementioned "Sexual Healing")—Columbia
Al Green: *Greatest Hits*—The Right Stuff/Capitol
Anything by Sade, anything by Barry White, Marvin Gaye, Van Morrison, Chris Isaak, Sting, and Luther Vandross

PROGRESSIVE AMBIENT

Massive Attack: *Mezzanine*—Virgin Records. Very dark, hypnotic and sexy, great for atmospheric striptease dancing!; *Blue Lines*—Virgin Records. A bit more upbeat and rhythmic

Ultra.Chilled—04—Ultra Records. A two-disc compilation set of hip, moody music, the fourth in their series

V.I.P. Lounge—Wagram/Virgin Records. Another two-disc compilation set, has some good sexy music to strip to

Portishead—*Dummy*—Polygram. Very dark and atmospheric, great for playing with a little light S&M!

Instant Karma—Warner Dance. A two-disc compilation imported from England that features artists like Groove Armada, Madonna, and Björk with classics like Beethoven's "Moonlight Sonata" and Dvorak's "New World Symphony"

WORLD

B-Tribe: *Fiesta Fatal!*—Atlantic. You'll want to get up and do a torrid flamenco dance for your man!

Romantica—Putumayo. Compilation of World Beat and Latin music

SOUTH ASIAN (SOMETIMES CALLED BHANGRA)

Arabic Lounge—Beechwood Music, Ltd. A two-disc compilation and a wonderful introduction to this newest form of world music

LATIN

Stan Getz and Antonio Carlos Jobim: *Getz/Gilberto*—Verve. Probably anything by Antonio Carlos Jobim

CLASSICAL

Prelude to a Kiss: Romantic Tunes—Rhino Records. A compilation that includes such romantic classics as Debussy's "Clair de Lune" and Puccini's theme from *Madame Butterfly*

Aria: A Passion for Opera—EMI Classics. Rich with famous romantic arias

The Most Relaxing Classical Album in the World Ever—Virgin

Records. A two-disc compilation set with wonderful classics like Mozart's "Elvira Madigan," Delibe's "Flower Duet," and Beethoven's "Moonlight Sonata."

Ravel's "Bolero"—Could I possibly leave that out? Think Bo Derek in the movie *10*.

Placido Domingo with John Denver: *Perhaps Love*. A real mood setter according to my friend, sex therapist Diana Wiley, who also raves about *The Best of Paolo Conte*. I'll have to go out and find these now!

BONUS SUGGESTIONS:
FOR ATMOSPHERIC WARM-UP MUSIC FOR THAT
ROMANTIC HOME-COOKED MEAL:

Dinner at Eight—Pottery Barn. You'll want your man to get up, pull out your chair for you, and sweep you up to your feet for a quick pas de deux.

Soundtracks with a Twist—Rhino Records. A bit campier compilation of such retro hits as Nelson Riddle's "Lolita Ya Ya" and the theme from *A Man and a Woman*

STRIPTEASE MUSIC

Martini Madness—Rhino Records. For those of you with a sense of humor and a love of camp, this has really fun priceless hits perfect to strip to, like Ann Margret singing "Thirteen Men," Mel Tormé singing "Comin' Home Baby," and Quincy Jones's "Soul Bossa Nova."

Putting in place the best lighting and music for the particular mood of a film is paramount for any good film director. As you prep the set of your sexual scenario, keep in mind the subtle but powerful force music and lighting can add to making your scene come alive. In the next chapter, you will see how location also plays a big role in how your sexual scenario unfolds.

Chapter 5

Sex on Location

Body of a woman, white hills, white thighs,
you look like a world, lying in surrender.
My rough peasant's body digs in you
And makes the son leap from the depth of the earth.
—Pablo Neruda, from "Body of a Woman"

Location, Location, Location

It's wonderful when you know your lover so well that you can get each other hot in two seconds flat. This kind of intimate knowledge about your partner is powerful and helps to develop a deep core of comfort between the two of you, which in turn can produce the absolute best sex ever. On the other hand, too much reliance on comfort and routine can make sex lose its thrill and luster. It becomes a predictable event, one that threatens to become a mere release or an obligatory marital duty. As a result, I'm always cautioning people that having sex the same way in the same place at the same time, day after day, is a surefire way to create boredom in the bedroom—one of the biggest causes of marital discord. Once couples fall into the rut of relegating sex to the last thing they do before falling off to sleep or a quickie in the morning, they run the danger of turning what was once a highlight of their relationship into a routine, mechanical afterthought.

It's not easy to keep the sex in a long-term relationship inventive and eventful. But it's also not impossible. If you want your union to remain sexy and inspiring, it's up to both of you to make the effort. One way to light a spark in a flagging fire is by consciously changing locations once in a while and not relying on your bed or bedroom as the only place to have sex. One couple I know told me that at least once a month, they bar themselves from the bedroom, and alternate seducing each other in a new place in their house. Some of their secret encounters took place on top of the washing machine in their laundry room, outside on their back deck, across the picnic table, and in the front hall closet. And while they said each place held its own allure and discomfort, the mere change in place was exciting.

By becoming a bit adventurous yourself by planning a sexual encounter in a place that is out of the ordinary, you can quickly fan the flames of desire and satisfaction. Most of us have fantasies of having sex in unexpected places. Haven't you wished your lover would grab you and take you right there—in the kitchen or the bathroom or the attic? Have you ever wanted to come up behind your lover and start to seduce him—while you're visiting him in his office? The sheer energy of the moment screams "I want you! I must have you—now!" What could be more of a turn-on than your lover being unable to control himself?

So what kinds of locations can we seek out to break the routine of day-to-day sex? There are two key elements that should be considered: one is inspiration, the other is comfort. Is there ample room, space? Things to lean on? If we get tired of standing, can we sit or lie down somewhere? There's nothing worse than developing a sudden cramp in your leg while you're in the throes of ecstasy.

It's just as important to choose or create a setting that inspires us to want to make love with our partner. This doesn't mean you have to become an interior designer or a magician; it simply means you need to think out of your sexual box—once in a while. Below I've listed some ideas that just might jump-start your sexual creativity.

Hotel Havens

The first and most obvious location outside your home is a hotel room. Depending on your budget or particular fantasy, this could mean anything from the famous Plaza Hotel in New York, with its sumptuous decor and flawless room service, to an off-the-beaten-path motel with its promise of secrecy and anonymity. My beau loves the idea of going to a hotel, even in our own city, and I have to admit I share his fondness. There's something sexy about going to a hotel for sex, a sense of the forbidden, and it's a great way to change the setting and give our lovemaking a whole new flavor. It's also great for inspiring all sorts of fantasies like the tried-and-true bar pickup or call-girl routine. Or the gigolo routine now that career women are calling the shots. Hotels and motels have also been a great escape for married couples with children who long to make love without fear of being interrupted by little Johnny's bad dream or need to pee. Hire that babysitter, get your mother-in-law over there, do whatever you have to do to buy yourself a night of uninterrupted, unbridled passion! Not everyone has to let the arrival of children mean the departure of a great sex life.

A Rendezvous on the Beach

The beach is a very popular setting that conjures up all sorts of romantic imagery. Think Burt Lancaster and Deborah Kerr in *From Here to Eternity* and the old early sixties sizzler *A Summer Place* and release all your fantasies of walking along the beach with your lover and stopping for an embrace that turns into a fit of uncontrollable desire. Or imagine climbing up the lifeguard chair to steal a kiss and who knows what else. I grew up on beach fantasies. As a young woman, I walked along the beach hand in hand with boyfriends imagining all sorts of romantic rendezvous. I finally got to try sex on the beach as an adult and was happily amazed at the result—despite what you may have heard about the dangers of getting sand where it would be most painful. If you're prepared, the beach can be a great location for romantic sex. The key is having enough blankets to completely wrap yourselves up inside so that no sand gets in between the two of you. Best of all is a sleeping bag. But if you prefer spontaneity and don't have a stash of blankets or a sleeping bag with you, I'd say go ahead and get started on the beach, but save the final act for when you get into a clean dry place—perhaps even the backseat of your car. The same rule of thumb applies when you're at a public beach or a private one that's heavily patrolled. My lover and I had to be on the lookout for the police occasionally patrolling the beach and that can certainly put a damper on the mood. Or, then again, maybe you're titillated by the thought of getting caught. Just be prepared for the consequences if you *do* get nabbed!

Sexy Spots Close to Home

So where are the more practical places where we can still get a kick out of doing it? An obvious one is the bathtub, particularly if it's not one of those New-York-City apartment-size tubs where one person can barely stretch out, let alone two. The challenge of a smaller tub is choosing who gets stuck on the side with the faucet poking into his back. Providing you're not stuck with a tiny tub, long luxurious baths together can be a great way to linger and play and sensually wash and caress each other. Set out some candles, choose your favorite bubble bath crystals (watch out for bath oils, they can make for some slippery and dangerous moves!), light some incense, and linger in the warmth and sensuality of soft fragrant caresses.

STAY WET AND WILD

One word of advice: keep some of your favorite lubricant around in case the water washes away some of those necessary lubricating juices. The best lubes that don't wash away are the silicon-based ones, but again, be careful as they do not break down in water and can create a very slippery environment. Watch your step when you're getting out of the tub!

Hot tubs are a great place to linger, especially under the stars. I've had friends who tell me of cold wintry nights under the stars where the steamy heat of the hot tub combines with their mutual lust to make for some very hot, romantic sessions.

The spontaneity of the kitchen can also be lots of fun. I have a scene in *Bridal Shower* where two friends are cooking together and one gives another a taste of what she's cooking when it drops right onto her breast. This inspires the friend to lick it off and turns their cook fest into a fun and erotic taste fest, in which they end up smearing food all over each others' breasts and bodies. The kitchen provides all sorts of possibilities for sex: leaning on the counters, lying on the kitchen table, using the chairs as props. And there's something oh so sexy about doing it in a place not designed or meant for sex. Just imagine donning an apron and playing out the French maid scenario as the master of the house comes home, or the *mistress* of the house returning from a hard day's work to find her houseboy cooking up a big luscious meal for her. Yum!

In my movie *Three Daughters*, the father finds his wife, wonderfully played by Gloria Leonard, up in the attic looking through the kids' old toys and reminiscing about their daughters who are all leaving home to begin their own lives. The wife happens to find an old pair of high heels she used to wear when they were dating and tries them on for him. "You always had the most beautiful legs," he tells her. "In fact, you still have the most beautiful legs." So begins a hot and tender scene during which they rediscover their passion for one another. You might plan on having your mate find you someplace unusual in the house when he comes home from work. You never know what might get inspired—especially if you just happen to be dressed up in some sexy little outfit. (See the next chapter for planning your wardrobe.)

DIRECTOR'S NOTE

One particularly torrid sexual encounter of mine took place in the stairwell of a commercial warehouse in the meatpacking district of New York City—*before* that area became chic, when it was still gritty and cutting edge. I was on a date with a sexy photographer whom I had known for some time but had only just begun dating. I was in an elegant long black coat and dress and the chemistry between us was palpable. Before we even made it up to his loft/studio, he grabbed me and pushed me down onto the stairs, bending me over and taking me right there from behind. The juxtaposition of me in my elegant black attire being taken on these rather grimy stairs was an incredible turn-on for both of us. It may not have been conducive to a long sensual session of lovemaking, but it certainly inspired us to continue once we got upstairs to his place!

Short of finding exotic locales and unusual places, you can also create a feeling of the unusual right in your own home. Redecorate your basement to resemble that of a sexy photo studio and become the model of your mate's dreams. Or turn your functional bedroom into a dungeon with accoutrement that can be hidden behind the headboard or under the mattress, with toys hidden in the back of the closet. With a little imagination, there's no end to what you can create out of the simplest or most functional of rooms.

If you're in a long-term relationship, think back to when you couldn't keep your hands off each other and how you'd simply grab each other and do it right then and there. And don't fall into the rut of having sex in the safety and comfort of your own bedroom. Try and recall some of the ways and places you used to have sex back then, and re-create the scene. You just might rediscover that same level of passion still lying in wait for your lover.

ROMANTIC GETAWAYS

The following suggestions come from both me and an informal poll of friends whom I know to be lovers of romantic travel:

- The Post Ranch; Big Sur, California: Pricey but luxurious with a Jacuzzi and a fireplace in every room
- Deetjen's Big Sur Inn; Big Sur, California: A very cozy, atmospheric, and less expensive alternative in Big Sur
- The Hotel Bellagio; Las Vegas: A cultured ambience in a glitzy world
- The Red Lion Inn; Stockbridge, Massachusetts: great for those autumn leaf-peeping getaways
- Heritage House Inn; Mendocino, California: Site for the movie *Same Time, Next Year* with Alan Alda and Ellen Burstyn
- Mauna Lani Resort and Bungalows; Big Island, Hawaii: A "very special place" according to my friend, sex therapist Diana Wiley, Ph.D.
- Tensing Pen; Negril, Jamaica: An amazing collection of unique wood, thatch, and cut-stone cottages, some on stilts overlooking the water
- Hotel de la Poste; Beaune, France: The original post office for this beautiful quaint village in the heart of the French Burgundy region, now a lovely hotel with a five-star restaurant
- Lizard Island: Australia's northernmost resort island near the Great Barrier Reef and the Blue Lagoon

CHIC/COOL HOTELS

New York City: The Mercer, 60 Thompson
Miami: The Delano
Caribbean: The Cotton House, Mustique
Paris: Montalambert, Pershing Hall
Rome: Es, The Hassler, de Russe

GOOD INTERNET SITES

Historic Inns of America (luxurious inns and bed-and-breakfasts)
BBonline.com (for bed-and-breakfasts)

RECOMMENDED BOOKS

Hip Hotels USA, Herbert Ypma, published by Thames & Hudson
Europe's Wonderful Little Hotels and Inns 2003: Continental Europe,
   Adam Raphael and Caroline Raphael (volumes for other
   countries as well), Steerforth Press
Dream Sleeps: Castle and Palace Hotels of Europe, Pamela L. Barrus
   and Carole T. Meyers, Carousel Press

Cautionary Tales

As an erotic filmmaker, I must go out of my way to present sex in
new and creative ways in every film in order to engage and enter-
tain my viewers. After all, I'm in the business of creating fantasy
images for people, not just showing people what they're able to do
themselves day after day. Therefore, I sometimes show lovers having sex in unusual places that in reality are not all that great.
There's a lot of mythology around doing it in so-called exotic
places that when tried out for real just don't hold up. Perhaps I
should present these scenes with a disclaimer "Don't try this at
home."

One that comes to mind is the dressing-room seduction in *One
Size Fits All.* While the scene is hot, hot, hot!, in reality trying to
have sex in a tiny cubicle measuring about three by three feet does
not leave much room for comfort and variety, not to mention the
risk of being discovered by other customers or staff. The same
goes for the scene in *Stud Hunters,* in which the two lovers are having sex standing up against the soundboard in a recording studio.
While the idea of wanting someone so badly you'll do it anywhere
is quite delicious, you need to know the reality of making this
scene: it was stifling hot, and the actors had to stand the whole
time. You should also know that most music producers would
probably freak at the thought of messing up their multi-thousand-
dollar soundboard.

Perhaps the most unlikely of all the scenes we've ever shot was the one in *Christine's Secret,* in which Christine's secret lover comes upon her on a swing and she manages to perfectly swing herself right onto him, wrapping her legs around his shoulders so that he can perform oral sex on her in this dreamlike, bucolic setting. While this scene actually won the Ladies Choice Award that year, it's likely to remain a wonderful fantasy idea rather than something one might actually try re-creating. Remember, most of my actors are what I call "sexual athletes"; it's their job to stay in superior physical shape and perform sexual feats that most of us could never manage to pull off.

On the personal front, I've had a few of my own disasters in attempting to make love in unusual places. The funniest thing that ever happened to me was when my ex-husband and I, while visiting his native Sweden, thought it would be romantic to make love in the woods. We stripped down and got hot and heavy pretty fast when suddenly we realized we were being attacked by a bunch of flies and "no-see-ums" attracted to the scents of lovemaking. Horrified, we pulled our clothes back on and fled! Same thing happened to me with a lover at his home in Ireland. Suddenly he felt flies landing on and nibbling his perspiring back and butt, at which point he grabbed his clothes and ran back in the house. He was so freaked out he couldn't even pick up where we had left off.

The lesson learned? Not all outdoor settings are truly that conducive to romance. On the other hand, I have shot an occasional scene outdoors with great success, such as the lovely picnic scene in *Bridal Shower.* I'm thinking that it might have been because of the season. It was March in Malibu and perhaps the insect population hadn't hatched yet! So if you are looking to play out that "me Tarzan you Jane" scenario or plan an erotic picnic, perhaps you should consider what time of year it is and do a little research into the current insect situation.

DIRECTOR'S   NOTE

Don't try sex in these places:

○ A moving vehicle

○ On a beach without a blanket underneath you

○ In a closet with the door shut

○ On naked ground near insects

○ Bathroom of an airplane

Another failed but ultimately comical attempt at exotic locations for me and my ex-husband was in the car. He had been on a film shoot in L.A. early on in our marriage and after a two-month separation, I flew out from New York to spend the Thanksgiving holiday with him. Since he was sharing a room with another crew member, searching for privacy we headed up into the Hollywood hills in the big old car he was using and thought it would be fun and racy to have sex right there in the big front seat. No sooner had we gotten into it when we felt the brightness of a flashlight on us. It was the cops. I couldn't believe that here I was, thirty-three and married, being busted for having sex in the car *with my husband!* It turned out we were in a highly private and patrolled area of Los Angeles. We had big laughs over that for years to come, but boy did we feel foolish at the time! Moral of the story? If you want to re-create those old days of being a young person with nowhere to go for illicit sex but the car, at least look for an area away from houses that's unlikely to be patrolled by the police.

Another no-no is the infamous mile-high club. Don't know what that is? In order to be a member of the mile-high club you must have sex on an airplane. This was again with my ex-husband when sex was new and hot and we couldn't keep our hands off each other. We had consumed a few drinks and wanted to do something naughty, so we crammed ourselves into the tiny airplane bathroom for a quickie. While we didn't get caught or anything, I'd have to say that that was probably one of the most uncomfortable settings I've ever attempted sex in my life. And with today's heightened security I'd have to say that it's definitely not worth the risk or the effort.

In general, I would be very careful of having sex in public places. While many people love the thrill and danger of getting caught, be careful where you choose to do this. While it may seem like fun and daring play, upsetting people is not fun and can get you into serious trouble. Again, in my films I will sometimes show couples sneaking a quickie in such places as a house being shown to them by a real estate agent, as in *The Gift*, or, in my darkest comedy scene ever, a funeral parlor in *My Surrender*. But these settings are definitely inappropriate for an intimate tryst. Not long ago two DJs at a top radio station in New York looking for ratings ran a contest challenging people to have sex in the most outrageous public place while they had a camera crew secretly taping them. One couple hit the jackpot when they did the deed at the back of St. Patrick's Cathedral on Fifth Avenue. They also landed themselves in court for lewd and indecent public behavior, the DJs lost their show, and the radio station had to jump through many legal hoops not to be taken off the air.

In another cautionary tale, I have a scene in my early Femme movie *Urban Heat*, in which an older woman seduces a young man in a freight elevator. While this turned out to be an unbelievably hot scene, it was inspired by a famous event that did not turn out as well. According to my ex-father-in-law, who's been in the film business for many, many years, a story once went around that the legendary movie star Rita Hayworth, at the top of her game at the time, seduced a young elevator operator in the elevator of an exclusive Paris hotel. The proprietors were not amused and proceeded to expel her from the hotel. Once again, leave it to fantasy, folks! The reality may prove to be far less than satisfying.

Now that you've selected your sexy and *safe* location for putting your script into action and creating your own love scene, it's time to move on to one of the truly major details: what will you, the star of your private movie, wear?

Chapter 6

Your Wardrobe

That's quite a dress you almost have on.
—Alan Jay Lerner, *An American in Paris*

From Clotheshorse to Vixen

I 've always been a clotheshorse. In high school, where I majored in fashion illustration, I would sketch in my private diary the outfit I was planning to wear the next day. To this day, I am still into clothes and fashion, and believe in their power to excite and make a dramatic impact on those around you. Of course, this is true in films as well as in life. The wardrobe of the actors during a film helps bring their characters further alive, capturing part of their personality and making a dramatic statement. But clothes are just as important in life *and* sex. After all, you can't be naked all the time.

In the movies I direct, I always include beautiful clothing, night-clothes, and especially underclothes for the women to wear as they begin their seduction. In one film, *One Size Fits All*, the whole plot hinges upon a sexy dress that kept finding its way into several women's wardrobes. It's a lavender spandex number with cord lac-ing—a very extreme garment that is meant to be funny and sexy at the same time. "This dress really works!" one of the women tells her girlfriends. She means, of course, that she always ends up having incredible sex when she wears this special dress with a lover. We all like to have special outfits—whether it's the quintessential little black dress or a racy sheath that we squeeze ourselves into—when we really want to wow someone. Thus the power of clothes.

WARDROBE ESSENTIALS

- A black dress—either cocktail style, a sheath, or in a wrap-style made famous by Diane von Furstenberg.
- Black pants—pants can be made of leather, wool crepe, rayon, or Lycra-cotton blend. Choose the fabric and style that suits your body.
- Black skirt—a simple elegant skirt can be very versatile. Depending on your particular style, and especially your legs, it can be floor length, midcalf, knee length, or mini.
- Tight black or white sweater—choose the style that best sets off your eyes, your neck, or your cleavage. Is it a turtleneck? A cowl neck that hints at your neck? A classic jewel collar? Or a plunging V-neck?
- Something, anything, in chiffon—a blouse, dressy pants, a scarf—this fabric is always romantic.
- A wrap—whether it's in rayon, silk, or pashmina, a wrap adds an elegance to your attire.

Wardrobe Equals Transformation

The true magic of clothes and lingerie is their ability to transform you into anything you want to be. If you want to look like a nasty hooker for your man, no problem. Just pick out the nastiest black lingerie and tall "come-fuck-me pumps" and you're transformed. Do you want to look like an innocent virgin ready to be taken? Then choose a pure white ensemble with layers of lingerie to be peeled off as you're seduced. Is an elegant seductress more your style? Go for a tasteful outfit made of pure silk with a flowing floor-length wrap that teasingly covers up the garments underneath. Or perhaps you want to be a gypsy goddess adorned in flowing silks and beaded headdress with bracelets and earrings that tinkle sweetly as you dance before your man. With a little creativity, we all have the power to transform ourselves and set the tone for an evening of romance and great sex. Were this not true, fashion wouldn't be such a huge industry and movies would not spend amply on wardrobe and costume designers.

In my movie *Three Daughters*, the youngest daughter, Heather, who is just discovering her blossoming sexuality and about to embark on her first love affair, sneaks into her sister's room and rifles through her ample collection of lingerie. We watch as Heather tries one ensemble on after another until she finally settles on a lovely white satin number that makes her look both beautiful and pure. Suddenly, she is transformed—like a "ripe peach ready to be plucked" as my older sister used to describe me way back when. There she stands, before a full-length mirror, looking like Botticelli's Venus, admiring herself as she realizes she is indeed becoming a woman.

DIRECTOR'S NOTE

I often insert little subtle bits of what I call everyday humor into my scenes, and in this case I added a touch that I'm sure went right over most people's heads. To show her true innocence in the scene in which she first makes love to her boyfriend, and at a time when she's trying hard to look like a woman who knows, I had the actress wear her panties under her garter belt. As any woman knowledgeable in the art of lingerie knows, panties must be worn *over* the garter belt if she wants to be able to remove her panties while still wearing her garters and stockings!

Of course, how you choose to transform yourself from everyday woman to temptress should also take into account what your man likes. When I prepared for my sexy striptease performance early on in my relationship with my current beau, I asked him what sorts of lingerie he likes to see on a woman. Being a pretty hip guy, he prefers to see me wear slightly more modern undergarments, like thongs and thigh-highs, rather than the traditional garters and stockings. But not all men even care for lingerie or have much use for it. One man I dated for a while would just say, "Wow," and then rip it off me in seconds. The costume meant nothing to him. I enjoyed my next boyfriend more, because he lingered over the phase of appreciating me in the outfit. He would run his hands up and down me and start making love to me while I was still wearing it. Perhaps my favorite is a man who enjoys buying and selecting lingerie for me.

Lingerie Equals Foreplay

Remember my sexy jazz musician? Another one of his stellar attributes was his impeccable taste in lingerie. He loved buying the most beautiful outfits for me. He frequented a shop on the Upper West Side of New York City, where the salesladies were grandmotherly Puerto Rican women who admired his determination to get the perfect gift for his girlfriend. "When I'm shopping for this stuff," he told me once, "it's almost as if I'm making love to you already." I still think to this day that foreplay began for him at that shop, where he imagined what I was going to look like in each outfit he carefully picked out. For me the foreplay began when I was presented with this lovely personal gift. One weekend we went away to a little bed-and-breakfast upstate, where he drew a bubble bath for me in the late afternoon. He washed me, caressing my entire body and taking photographs of me in the tub. Then he brought in the outfit and left me to get dressed. Having this sensuous sexy man as my wardrobe master was wonderful, and knowing that he had been in that lingerie shop letting other women know that he was very much in love with me also turned me on. The sex we had after the bath was so hot that I'm sure we interrupted the other guests during their dainty little afternoon tea as we tumbled off the bed in the heat of passion and shook the chandeliers below.

As you will see even more explicitly in chapter 7, the anticipation of sex is often a crucial phase of arousal for a woman, and that's what creating a wardrobe taps into: your arousal factor. It is also why I like to include scenes in my films of women planning for sexual adventures, such as in the scene I described earlier from *Three Daughters*. Selecting your wardrobe, all the way down to what goes underneath, can be a wonderful part of the process of planning a sexy evening when you use clothes to enhance your body. Just as costume design is crucial to any good movie, so is designing your personal wardrobe when it comes to planning your own private scene. And don't forget to pick something out for afterward. Just because you've finished making love doesn't mean you can throw that old tattered chenille robe on. Make sure you have the perfect little cover-up to slip into.

Becoming Your Own Award-Winning Costume Designer

Making your wardrobe work for you means finding clothes— whether lingerie or an outfit—that make you feel sexy and able to project this sexual confidence to your man. Many a man has told me there is nothing sexier to a man than a sexually confident women. By the same token, there's also nothing worse than a woman sandwiched into an outfit that's absolutely wrong for her. I recall learning that sometimes painful lesson during my very first appearance in an adult film. It was a small, low-budget shoot that I accepted just to see if I could handle doing that kind of work. I arrived with a cute navy and cranberry paisley print minidress with bell sleeves, so stylish for the times—circa 1975. I was handed a pair of navy blue thigh-highs—something I had never worn before. I always had full thighs, especially when I was still carrying a bit of baby fat, and once I got those thigh-highs on I was horrified by how I looked. In those days the elastic bands were quite thin and prone to slipping down the leg. I felt like my thighs resembled squished sausages oozing out of the tops of their too-tight casings. Not conducive to feeling comfortable in my first ever role in a blue movie (an adult film).

This experience taught me an important lesson: don't wear something just because some reed-thin model looks great in it. Wear what enhances what you've got. We've all got something special to flaunt. Show off those parts and learn to camouflage the parts you don't like.

A Sexy Outfit Doesn't Mean Skintight

The seventies were notorious for getting women to squeeze into the tightest spandex clothes we could find, and these days it isn't much easier with fashions that highlight exposed midriffs that cut as far down as you can go without showing your pubic hair. But if you notice, the gals that can get away with that stuff are mostly under thirty. And that's fine when we're puppies in heat, discovering our sexuality and flaunting it for all the world to see. As we get older we learn the art of subtlety and sophistication—at least we *should*! My twenties were a nonstop exercise in fashion faux pas, starting off with my feminist hippie days where I rejected everything fashionable and wore nothing but denim bell-bottoms and poor boy sweaters (which was actually kind of a sexy look for that time. I even got criticized by the PC [politically correct] patrol for looking too sexy!). Then I moved to San Francisco and discovered the riotous campy look of the drag queens I was hanging out with.

We all dressed in forties and fifties clothes picked up for pennies at the local thrift stores.

When I moved to L.A. and joined the ranks of the tacky spandex-wearing babes, I learned how to clomp around in those painfully high "come-fuck-me pumps" and had bikinis custom-made for me in bright orange to offset the turquoise swimming pools ever present in L.A. Can you imagine? I have to admit it was fun. But even more fun was my discovery of sexy lingerie. With stores such as Trashy Lingerie popping up in Hollywood, which took sexy undies further into the realm of camp and high fashion, it was easy to get hooked. Looking sexy was never more fun.

But growing out of our twenties and thirties doesn't have to mean the end of looking sexy. It might just mean learning the art of subtlety and camouflage as our bodies age and take on a mind of their own. One important lesson is that we do not have to wear skintight clothes to look sexy. In fact, sometimes the suggestion or hint of what's underneath is far sexier and more enticing than letting it all hang out in the first place. Clothes that glide along the body, hinting at curves and suggesting the womanly shape that lies beneath can be far more elegant and appealing, especially in up-scale settings. The little black dress is not meant to expose every nook and cranny of your body; it's supposed to tease and entice with what it suggests.

I have come a long way since my days of wanting to shock and amuse with what I wear. I truly appreciate simplicity and form over ostentatiousness. A woman who chooses understated elegance over flaunting what she has is admired for her self-assuredness, taste, and sexual confidence. Men tend to want to get close to a woman who seems so self-assured. They want to know what she's hiding in there that makes her so confident. I must admit that there have been times that I have spent hours agonizing over what to wear; yet when I opt for something simple and black and elegantly sexy, I always get the best response from men. I recall one time showing up in a black floor-length Mandarin-style dress that buttoned all the way up to the neck. My date was so turned on he couldn't help but take me right then and there and even requested that I leave the dress on the whole time.

The same rule applies to lingerie. You don't have to squeeze into the tightest tiniest bra and panties to look good; nor do you have to put up with flimsy garter belts that dig into your flesh and keep slipping down your stomach. And a word about thongs: I know they're all the rage, even on some beaches. But if you don't have a well-toned butt to go along with the thong, only wear it under your clothes to avoid panty lines. Don't parade around in them in front of your man. Sorry, but you've got to have the fanny for thongs. There are plenty of wonderfully cut panties to choose from these days without making a fool of yourself. Try one of those wonderful new panties that sort of hug the hips in a V-shape giving you lots of lengthening thigh without exposing too much butt. I saw them listed as "stretch lace boy shorts" on Lingeriesite.com.

If you've got the kind of curves women are supposed to have, you probably won't look good in those minuscule pieces of cloth modeled by underage girls in all the fashion magazines that torture women with unrealistic and unattainable images. And don't think men *want* these kinds of girls either. Men want *women*, and they want women with flesh and curves to hold onto.

Lingerie to Make You Look and *Feel* Sexy!

Assuming you're not one of the lucky few who retains a thin girlish body past childbirth and the normal transformations of age, the most flattering types of lingerie to select are silky flowing peignoirs and camisoles. Even thin girls benefit from this type of lingerie. In another scene from *Three Daughters*, the middle daughter seduces her piano tutor. This actress, a law student from Israel, was exceptionally thin and we decided she would look sexier with her cream-colored teddy left on. Eventually the top fell to her waist and the actor entered her by pushing aside the crotch panel. From this highly erotic scene, I learned that there really is something almost sexier about a woman being made love to half undressed rather than completely naked. So once you do select your perfect enhancing lingerie don't feel like you have to completely remove it.

My personal favorite style of lingerie is the baby-doll look, possibly a holdover from my love of fifties and early sixties clothes. It conjures up images for me of Sandra Dee and Doris Day in all those silly romantic comedies of that era. I have an original pale pink baby doll with layers of very fine silky fabric that just glide over my full breasts and float down over my middle ending right across my midthighs in the most teasing way. It really makes me feel like a naughty vixen! And if I happen to have eaten a big meal or am having one of those unwelcome days of bloating, I know I'm still looking cute and sexy without having to worry about my middle.

Lingerie can also be elegant while camouflaging a less-than-perfect hourglass figure. A floor-length ensemble made of fine silk can be amazingly alluring and oh so kind to all those little bumps and valleys we prefer to hide. Slink back on a chaise lounge and cross your legs in a gown with a slit up the side and you will look like an absolute goddess. You don't have to remove it either. Just let him slide the matching panties down your legs and take you like that. There's something oh so naughty about the idea of taking a woman who's still wearing her clothes—or her elegant dressing gown.

You don't have to opt for being covered up either. There are a growing number of clothing lines and catalogs that cater to the full-bodied woman. You can pick from an array of slinkier underthings that are cut more fully making you both comfortable and sexy even in garters and stockings. The fashion world is finally recognizing that most women do *not* resemble the Victoria's Secret models and are creating luscious varieties of undergarments for women with womanly figures. I will list some of them in my resources list.

There are an amazing and still growing variety of sensuous and alluring styles of lingerie to choose from, whether you're a diminutive waif or a voluptuous goddess. So don't shy away from the transformative powers of seductive dress. Experiment and play and surprise your man with a whole new you!

WARDROBE DO'S AND DON'TS

DO:

- Choose an outfit that stimulates your sensual appetite and suits your mood.
- Select clothing that fits and enhances your body.
- Experiment with various styles of lingerie until you find the piece or pieces that stir(s) you—and your man—the most.
- Err on the side of elegant versus revealing. By and large, most men prefer a classy fashion to the bodice-ripping look.

DON'T

- Squeeze yourself into a skintight outfit.
- Overdress for the occasion.
- Wear your five-inch heels to a restaurant or for a romantic stroll.
- Dress in styles that don't suit you.

Uncomfortable Is Not Sexy

Just as garter belts that dig into your thighs and slide down your tummy can be unflattering as well as uncomfortable, so can some of those corsets that look so great on the store mannequin. If you're going to go for one, try and get a piece that isn't so tight that you won't be able to move or take a bite of food without developing a stomachache. Of course some women love squeezing into those elaborate corsets that tie in the back and pull our waists into unrealistic and painful proportions. (Think Scarlett O'Hara in *Gone With the Wind*.) They may be fun for dress-up, but have you ever tried to make love in one of those things? The last movie I appeared in back in 1980 (and also wrote—hints of things to come!) was a turn-of-the-century period piece called *Blue Magic* in which all of us were outfitted in authentic clothes from that era. That meant Gibson hairdos for the actresses and authentic corsets that took two people to tie you in. I can tell you that we couldn't even *sit* in that gear—let alone make love. No wonder the Victorian era was notorious for sexual repression—except for all the men who frequented prostitutes, of course.

Also among the world's most uncomfortable garments are those ultratight latex dresses many of us wore in the eighties and nineties. I owned two, one in red and one in silver, and they made me look great. No wonder Marlene Dietrich liked to wear tight body suits to contain her flesh; they fit like girdles, pulling everything in and holding it in for as long as you can take it. But I could only wear latex outfits for public appearances. Nothing made out of latex is truly sexy because it's nearly impossible to wriggle out of. You must put powder all over your body to even get the thing on and then the unbreathable material traps your sweat against your skin, kind of like those old gimmicky plastic suits that were supposed to make you lose weight because they made you sweat so much.

Here's my advice: save the latex numbers for show and wear something more accessible if you want to be seduced. There's nothing less sexy than struggling and contorting your body in order to wriggle out of one of those things. Believe me, I've done it and it's *not* a pretty sight. Again, the dreaded sausage-casing image comes to mind. Plus, you're drenched in sweat from spending all evening in this unnatural sheath. Latex is strictly fantasy and an uncomfortable reality. But if you really want to have the experience of wearing latex, or your man wants you to dress up in it, you might want to think about undressing in private and taking a nice fragrant shower before he takes you to bed. On the other hand, if he's looking to be dominated by a latex-clad vixen then perhaps none of this matters. Just leave on the latex until you're done giving him what he deserves and then slip into the shower, leaving him to lick his wounds.

Sexy Alternatives to Lingerie

Not every man likes the look of traditional lingerie. There have been years during which my vast collection of lingerie lay dormant and unused because a current beau was not into that sort of thing. Some guys go wild over a woman in a white T-shirt and jeans, and I've known plenty of men who love seeing their ladies in plain white cotton panties. I even have one friend who insists that his woman wear white sweat socks for him. Apparently this sort of preference has a lot to do with what he was exposed to when his young hormones kicked in during puberty.

My friend recounts the story of how he used to bend down to the floor to look under the big divider that separated the girl's gym from the boy's gym, and all he could see were the girls' ankles running around in sweat socks and sneakers—hence his later penchant for women in sweat socks. So if your sex life is doing just fine and your man seems happy and content, don't feel like you have to alter your style to spice up your sex life—just enhance it. Chances are the man you're trying to please was attracted to you because of your look, and if you're a jeans and T-shirt type of girl who suddenly goes Victoria's Secret, you could find the results less than rewarding.

Even Panty Hose Can Be Sexy

Every woman knows that panty hose are much more comfortable than garter belts and stockings, and most of us under fifty grew up wearing them. Some men aren't able to see panty hose as erotic because they've traditionally fallen into the practical underwear category. In fact some men curse the day they were invented. These men tend to be of a certain age in which the women with whom they grew up were still donning everyday garters and stockings; that's what came to define woman for them. That's also why most traditional porn movies featured garters and stockings at a time when women were no longer wearing them. You'll rarely see a woman wearing panty hose in an adult movie.

When I began directing movies, I was interested in a more realistic yet still sexy look, and took the chance of dressing some of my actresses in panty hose with great success. In *The Gift*, a husband and wife in their forties go house-hunting. There's a scene where the couple makes love upstairs after the Realtor leaves them alone. This scene cried out for panty hose for two reasons:

○ **Realism.** Of course the woman would be wearing panty hose under her dress. What normal woman in her forties would be wearing an elaborate garter belt setup on her way to a real estate open house?
○ **The actress had a great ass.** Panty hose can only emphasize a beautiful derriere. (Oddly enough, a nice pair of pull-up hose can camouflage imperfections too.)

In the scene in *The Gift*, I directed the handsome actor/husband to come up behind his wife. He lifts up her skirt so that her rear end is exposed, panty hose and all. Then he slowly peels the panty hose down her thighs. The scene is absolutely hot—and I've never had any complaints from any of my male viewers.

Gloria Leonard, a close friend and the costar of the classic *The Opening of Misty Beethoven*, agreed to be in my film *Three Daughters*, playing the mom. She wanted to wear a flowing dress to camouflage a few extra pounds around her middle, and under that she wore panty hose. Gloria was always known for her great legs, long and lithe, so we definitely wanted to play them up. In a tender scene where she and her husband rediscover their passion for each other, he comments on what beautiful legs she's always had and proceeds to literally tear through her panty hose so that he can go down on her. "Those were brand-new panty hose!" she cries out. "I'll buy you a new pair," he protests. "I'll buy you a box of them!" "Good!" she says happily. "I like this!" My then husband and producer came up with that idea and it was a great one.

A LITTLE TIP ABOUT PANTY HOSE

Save the pairs with runs and put them on for lovemaking. One of my lovers really enjoyed ripping them off my body, and what a happy compromise: I loved this fierce display of unbridled passion and they were already ruined anyway.

Panty hose don't have to be the plain, neutral-colored bores they used to be either. With today's varied offerings you can find sleek black hose that are sheer all the way up to the waist, hose with French-cut panty lines built into them, and some with elegantly sexy patterns up the leg, most notably those made by Wolcott, a British manufacturer that produces superior undergarments. My man loves the long look of my legs in a pair of black sheer-to-the-waist hose. In some ways my legs look even better than being cut up by the lines of stockings and garters, so sleek and shapely. And for a touch of naughtiness, try a pair of crotchless pantyhose. Last time I came out in a pair of those was in a Paris hotel last summer with my beau. Needless to say we never made it out to dinner that night!

These Boots Are *Not* Made for Walkin'

People frequently ask, "Why do women always keep their shoes on in pornographic movies?" Well, from a filmmaker's point of view, I can tell you that we have a lot of trouble keeping the actresses' feet clean on the set. There have been so many times when we've been about to shoot, and some production assistant has to run out and get a wet washcloth to tidy up the soles of my leading lady's feet. It happened all the time in my acting days too. If you have those fabulous high heels strapped to your arches, your feet stay clean. But, of course, cleanliness is not the only reason that adult films often feature naked women with shoes. Somehow, along the way, it became a convention for sexy protagonists to keep their shoes on while engaged in lovemaking.

A HISTORICAL PERSPECTIVE

The tradition of the naked woman with shoes goes way back to photographs of prostitutes from the late nineteenth century. Perhaps it's the female version of that old Western thing, "He died with his boots on." "She climaxed with her shoes on!" I suppose there is just something naughtier about being totally nude with the exception of your extremities.

Men have always adored and worshipped women's feet. The female foot has been eroticized for centuries in many cultures. The most extreme example is the foot binding of ancient China in which girls' feet were bound so that they were unable to grow and remained tiny. (I won't even go into the political ramifications of the helplessness of women who basically can't walk on their own two feet. Let's just be grateful we don't live in such times.) Men like to see women in high heels. And high heels can transform a woman's body and alter her gait. High heels lift the calves making them appear more shapely. They also make you lift up and stick out your butt, as well as thrust your breasts forward. When you don a sexy pair of heels, you feel different, walk differently, and you assume a certain attitude that just isn't there when you're wearing your more practical comfy shoes. Of course wearing high heels too often can cause you to develop painful bunions and foot problems that require surgery, so be careful about how often you traipse around in these impractical and potentially destructive things. In fact I often say that high heels should be strictly for the bedroom. If you have foot problems, just keep your "come-fuck-me pumps" for those most intimate times. Why walk in a scary pair of heels when you can enjoy them horizontally? As one of my friends says, "Wear shoes to spur them on!"

Not all men, however, are into women in high heels, at least not in bed. A woman can look adorable in running shoes or Rollerblades. Think Rollergirl in *Boogie Nights*. In the first erotic scene of my movie *Bridal Shower*, we see Sharon Kane's character going off on a picnic in the beautiful Malibu Canyon with a handsome young actor. She's wearing a long flowing flower-print dress, a wide-brimmed straw hat, and lace-up combat boots and sweat socks. While she strips down to her white lacy undies, she leaves her combat boots and socks on for the entire scene and it never detracts from her beauty. In fact, the practical boots and socks make her look cute and contemporary. I'm sure many women can relate: hey, I can wear clodhopper boots and still have a great sex life!

DEFINING FULL FIGURED

Contrary to what most fashion magazines would have us think, most women *are* full figured. I was surprised to learn from my local lingerie shop that the average bra size for American women is actually around a 36D. I was surprised to learn this fact because I live in New York City, where women make a sport of staying thin and the average bra size here is 34B and C. But in reality most women are a lot heftier than that. Let's hear it for the full figure!

CANDIDA CLOSE-UP

Q: I love looking through the latest Victoria's Secret catalog, but I always become frustrated. I am a large-size woman (size sixteen to be exact) and I never can find any sexy lingerie to fit me. Do you have any suggestions?

A: You should relish your full figure! There are many catalogs that cater to women who are full figured. One that is exceptional is called The Curvy Catalog, and you can reach it at the Web site SecretsinLace.com.

Putting It All Together

Putting together your wardrobe is a very personal, subjective experience—one that only you can decide on. Here is a round-up of my most essential advice when it comes to giving your sexual persona that extra dimension:

- ⊙ Lingerie is transformative, as are clothes. Allow yourself the freedom to let go and become the vixen you want to be. Be creative and play. The bedroom is the one place we get to be both playful and grown up. Go with it and most of all, have fun!
- ⊙ You don't always have to think in terms of lingerie. For instance, as I described in *Bridal Shower*, the character dons a cute flowing dress, straw hat, and combat boots, with only white undies underneath. Many men don't care for lingerie and they'll usually let you know. Women have many more options now, from the typical lacy garters and stockings ensemble to the simple contemporary cotton briefs look. What's on top of those undies has just as much potential to transform and tease.
- ⊙ Learn the art of subtlety and sophistication. As we get older we learn much more and have the clout to carry off whatever we choose to convey through our dress. Think in terms of elegant eroticism.
- ⊙ If you do opt for lingerie, remember to purchase and wear things that make you feel comfortable and sexy and desirable. To look good you have to feel good. Don't feel like you have to

stuff yourself into tiny, tight things that are meant for skinny models. There are so many options, like the soft sexy flowing baby dolls and long elegant silky gowns, all just as sexy—if not more!

○ There are lines of lingerie and catalogs now that cater specifically to the full-figured woman. Check them out and you'll see further proof that you don't have to be a model to look sexy and alluring (see the resources section at the end of the book).

○ As I did with my guy when prepping his private strip show, you can ask your man what kind of lingerie or underwear he likes. Better yet, if he's into that sort of thing, you can take him shopping with you. My guy loves taking me to his favorite little French lingerie boutique where he gets to sit and watch me try things on. It's like foreplay. And best of all, he loves buying me sexy lingerie, so *he* pays for whatever I choose!

○ Don't overlook panty hose. There are now lots of companies making panty hose that are truly sexy, ones that are sheer to the waist and others that have lines looking like French cut thongs rather than the practical ones that cut across your thighs. These new sexy styles actually can emphasize and accentuate the length of your legs and be quite sexy and elegant. And for that extra naughty look don't forget the crotchless ones!

○ You don't have to dress in clichéd ideas of what's sexy. Choose what makes *you* feel sexy and you *will* be sexy!

Now that you've got your wardrobe picked out and you're ready to transform yourself, it's time for the next step: prepping your equipment.

Chapter 7

Prepping Your Equipment

In Western medical tradition genital massage to orgasm by
a physician or midwife was a standard treatment of hysteria. . . . This purported disease and its sister ailments displayed a symptomology consistent with normal functioning
of female sexuality, for which relief, not surprisingly, was
obtained through orgasm.

—Rachel Maines, *Technology of Orgasm: "Hysteria," the Vibrator, and
Women's Sexual Satisfaction*

It's Playtime

As a director, I rely on my crew to prep my equipment and to
make sure everything works and works well—lights, cam-
eras, sound recording decks, electrical equipment. It's crucial that everything is working, glitch free, and ready to go when I
say "Action!" Thank God I'm not the one who has to worry about
prepping the equipment for my films. But when it comes to stag-
ing your own night of fabulous lovemaking, you are in charge.
What equipment am I speaking of? Well of course, your toys,
ladies! Whether you are a long-term aficionada of sexual toys, or
you are just getting started discovering these sexual playthings,
here are some suggestions for popular toys as well as some of my
favorites. I've also included some vital information on other basics, including lubes and condoms that are easy and safe to use.

All toys are products meant to enhance your sexual experience—they provide ways for you and your lover to have more fun,

increase your sensitivity and pleasure, and make sex last that much longer.

Toy Box Essentials

I assume that we all agree that women should always aspire to have fun—why not apply this same rule to sex? Remember the episode of *Sex and the City* in which Miranda realizes that her house cleaner discovered her special drawer of goodies? It's a known fact: any woman who's interested in keeping her sex life interesting and ful- filling must take the initiative and keep a well stocked, state-of-the- art supply of fun and functional sex toys and products, ensuring that she has what *she* likes to play with. So ladies, let's fill your toy box! These goodies should preferably be stored in a drawer or box within easy reach of the bed so as little interruption as possible takes place. And if you're concerned about someone such as your house cleaner or your kids or even your snoopy babysitter discov- ering your precious supply, find a way to keep your toy box locked or stashed in an unlikely place. My drawer of goodies is built into my platform bed and is very difficult to get to, due to its proximity to my dresser. I know *I* can get into it and keep my favorite items within easy reach, and that's all that matters.

So what should you have in your toy box? Here are some basics:

- a good lubricant or two
- condoms if you're in a new or noncommitted relationship and haven't yet presented each other with a clean bill of health and/or a method of contraception
- your favorite vibrator
- extra batteries if your vibrator is battery-operated
- your favorite dildo or other kind of toy for insertion
- any other toys you might like or want to experiment with, such as a harness, cock rings, or butt plug

○ a good book or two of sexy erotic stories
○ your favorite erotic videos

TIPS FOR KEEPING YOUR TOY BOX SECRET

○ Use a storage unit that locks with a key.
○ Place your toy box (or your toys) in a bedside drawer that locks.
○ Place your toy box in your closet when you are not using it—but remember to bring it out, preferably before the action begins.
○ Build a sliding shelf underneath your bed.

Talking Shop

Now let's talk shop about this equipment. Following are my recommendations and those of others I've surveyed.

Vibrators

Back around 1992 when I was exploring ways in which to expand my product line, I visited my friends at Good Vibrations, one of the first woman-friendly stores and mail order operations, based in San Francisco. They were kind enough to allow me to peruse their sales sheets. What I discovered to some surprise was that dildos and especially vibrators made up a full 40 percent of their sales. That's when I realized that *women want their vibes and dildos.* And with the growing level of comfort women are developing around their sexuality, the numbers are probably even higher now. Vibrators have come a long way since the cheap standard-issue plastic tapered vibe you placed discreetly against the woman's neck in those laughable ads—though I'm sad to say that most magazines still require such silly masquerades when it comes to advertising women's pleasure products. But never mind, we all know what they're really for. So let's explore some of the latest contributions to the world of pleasurable vibrations.

There are basically two types of vibrators, electric and battery-operated. Electrics tend to be much stronger. The most well known and popular electric vibrator is the Hitachi Magic Wand. Women who prefer or require a very strong sensation swear by this one and often find the battery-operated vibes to be insufficient. One suggestion, though: most sex counselors will advise women to place a light towel or dry folded washcloth between the Magic Wand and their clitoris in order to prevent overstimulation and desensitization. Being kind of a lightweight myself, I can recall some years ago putting one of those double-headed Hitachis (designed to fit around the back muscles) directly on my clitoris and almost hitting the roof. It was not pleasant! So if you're a first-time user you might want to heed this advice.

Battery-operated vibes might not be enough for the dedicated Magic Wand users, but they offer a wonderful variety of shapes and sizes and strengths for the rest of us to choose from. There are your standard lightweight plastic phallus-shaped vibes and many variations of the same; those with all kinds of funny animal heads that stick out and diddle your clitoris at the same time; some with little pearls that go round and round the middle to stimulate the inner walls of your vagina; and a growing number of "G-spotters." In fact my friend sex educator Jamye Waxman, who spent a year working at the popular woman-friendly shop in New York City, Toys in Babeland, tells me that curved vibes are currently the most popular right now, and that those made of plastic vibrate the strongest, except of course for electric vibes. Silicone vibes are very popular because they vibrate throughout the entire piece and they're not porous, which means no bacteria can get in. Many plastic vibrators are made of antibacterial materials and usually say so on the packaging.

An all-time favorite for many women is the Rabbit, which combines the little animal—the "rabbit"—that diddles your clitty while the shaft twirls around to stimulate your G-spot and a ring of tumbling pearls tickle the opening of your vagina. I had tried one awhile back and couldn't figure out what all the hoopla was about. However, I recently sampled another Rabbit and now understand why so many women like it. The sensations are delicious! My advice is to steer clear of the knockoffs, which I had apparently used the first time, and go for the real deal. How can you tell which is the authentic Rabbit? My friends at Toys in Babeland tell me they only carry the Vibratex because they think this model is the best; the Vibratex is also the one I tried. It *is* a costly item, around eighty-five dollars, but this is one case where the old adage you get what you pay for holds true.

Another common favorite is the Pocket Rocket due to its powerful punch in a small relatively nondescript package. My expert Jamye tells me the little Fukuoko vibe that fits on the finger is also a lot of fun and good for those who are nervous about bringing vibes into their partner play.

I would be remiss if I did not mention my own line of Natural Contours vibrators. I created this line with a brilliant young Dutch industrial designer back in the late nineties in order to answer the need for better quality and more discreet sexual products for women who wanted something that wasn't so blatantly phallus shaped and/or obviously sexual. In other words, something you could keep at home or travel with—without fear of discovery and embarrassment. But discretion wasn't their only plus; we also made them ergonomically correct, following the lines and contours of a woman's body for ultimate fit and comfort. I always found it puzzling that something that was meant to stimulate the clitoris was shaped like a phallus. Could it be because it was designed by a man??? Two of our models sit on the woman's pubic bone for direct clitoral stimulation, enabling the man to enter her at the same time if she so chooses. We also have a tiny waterproof model that packs a more powerful punch than the others, answering the need of those women who want more intense stimulation. But my personal favorite, and the first of its kind, is the Ultime, a U-shaped vibrator that actually stimulates both the clitoris *and* the G-spot! That's why I named it the "Ultime"—because it's the *ultimate!* What I particularly love about this vibrator is the warm sensation it gives inside my entire vaginal area.

Another popular G-spot vibrator to hit the market is called the Nubby G. I haven't tried it myself, but it seems to be a growing hit. And I hear women mention the Waterdancer a lot. It's described as powerful, compact, and waterproof.

For something that can also stimulate your guy, try the Orbit Ring Vibe. It's a stretchy, soft clear rubber ring that slides over the penis and testicles (also onto a dildo). It can be positioned to vibrate on the scrotum or for clitoral stimulation.

Before I leave the area of vibrators, I should mention the Eroscillator, endorsed by the grandmotherly Dr. Ruth, who helped make a generation of couples become more comfortable talking about sex. According to the description I found on the product's Web site, this toy is *not a vibrator.* Instead, it's said to provide a "totally unique, gentle 'oscillating' motion" that is "soft and natural, from side to side rather than up and down like a vibrator."

One more rather new item, something called the Eros, is actually approved by the FDA as a prescription device to treat female sexual dysfunction (FSD), caused by inadequate blood flow to the genital area. It works like a pump and fits over the clitoris like a suction cup, and engorges the clitoris with blood so that it improves both vaginal lubrication and sensation. There's a fair amount of debate within the women's sexuality field regarding what some call the "medicalization of women's sexuality." But if you feel you have a serious problem with achieving sexual satisfaction, you may want to look into the Eros. Be forewarned that I have never tried this product, nor do I know anyone who has.

Also, it's very expensive, not to mention you must have a doctor's prescription for it.

DIRECTOR'S NOTE ON VIBRATORS

I'm often asked whether one can become addicted to vibrators, especially the strong electric ones, resulting in loss of sensation or a dependence on them. My feeling is that if you don't *need* the heavy-duty strength of an electric vibe and get off fine with a battery-operated model, perhaps you should stick with the lesser strength. It's certainly possible that you could become a bit desensitized from using a strong vibrator and thus become unnecessarily reliant on it. If you don't need a vibrator at all, finding the softness of fingers and tongues adequate, you might not want to bother with one. But if you're one of the many women who prefers and enjoys the extra stimulation of a vibrator, whether it be a battery-driven lightweight or an electric one with a powerful kick, and especially if it's actually enabled you to achieve orgasm when all else fails, then why care if you become dependent on it? Whatever gets you off and brings you to that wonderful place of satisfaction is all that really matters.

THE FAMOUS G-SPOT

While some people still debate whether or not there is actually such a thing as a G-spot, many women, myself included, do find that they have an area just up inside the vagina, on the top side, that's extremely sensitive when stimulated and can make their orgasms extremely intense. In fact many women produce a female ejaculation by stimulating this area. I find that when both my clitoris and G-spot area are stimulated at the same time, my orgasms are unbelievably powerful and can go on much longer than if I stimulate only my clitoris. While the G-spot is neither an obvious button like the clitoris nor something immediately and easily definable to the naked eye, a little searching around inside there should help you locate the raised and rippled area referred to as the G-spot, after the German doctor Graffenberg. While I will include in my resource lists the names of some excellent videos available on the market that help women locate and explore their G-spot potential, one good place to start is with the book simply named *The G-Spot* by Dr. Beverly Whipple, who continues to do extensive research in this area.

PC MUSCLES: USE THEM OR LOSE THEM

We now know that the clitoris is not just that little button you see peeking out from under its hood at the top of your vulva. It's in fact part of the entire band of muscles that surrounds your vaginal area known as the PC (pubococcygeus) muscles. This large band of muscles forms the base of your pelvic floor and is rich with nerve endings, including the area commonly referred to as the G-spot. These muscles are what produce the intense contractions produced during orgasm. The condition of these muscles, which wrap all around the vaginal area, also determines the strength of your orgasms and what makes your pussy tight or loose. These muscles must be kept in shape just like any other muscles in the body. They can loosen and atrophy from both childbirth and age. If you're not sure which muscles I'm referring to, they are the ones that you clench when you have to stop the urge or flow of urine. You can also find these muscles by inserting a finger or two inside your vagina and contracting and then releasing.

It's important to keep these muscles toned and exercised if you want to have a tight pussy and strong, wonderful orgasms. Fortunately one way to keep your PC muscles strong and tight is by remaining sexually active and having regular orgasms. This is possible even if you're not in a current relationship. Simply masturbate yourself to orgasm and you've exercised your vaginal muscles. But it's not always that easy. If we've allowed our vaginal muscles to weaken and/or atrophy from childbirth or sexual inactivity, particularly after menopause, we must consciously exercise them by doing what are called kegels, which strengthen and tone the PC muscles. Once you've isolated and identified your PC muscles, the kegels are simple: squeeze as if you are trying to stop the flow of urine. Do repetitions of ten quick squeezes and then hold tightly for a count of ten, and then release. I repeat this exercise whenever I do my regular workout, between reps of weight lifting or cool-down periods. No one will know you're doing them so you can do them anywhere, even while sitting on the train or in your Pilates class!

Another way to exercise these muscles is with G-spot vibrators like my Natural Contours Ultime or with a vaginal barbell, which relies on the principle of resistance training. Some models come in stainless steel, like Betty's Barbell designed and distributed by Betty Dodson, aka the mother of masturbation. I've also recently created one for my Natural Contours line called the Énergie. They all weigh about a pound for resistance and come with instructions on how to use them. (I also happen to like using it on myself as a sort of "dildo" while masturbating myself to orgasm. The heavier weight and the rounded ends, like the head of a penis, make for some wonderful vaginal and G-spot stimulation while I come.) However you choose to strengthen and tone your PC muscles, the important thing is to do it, especially after you've given birth (vaginally) or if you're postmenopausal. Remember, the strength of your orgasms is in direct proportion to the strength and condition of your vaginal muscles, so *that* should certainly give you incentive. Not to mention the response of your man when he enters you and feels a nice tight pussy.

Dildos

I've never understood why such a fantastic little invention had to have such a crude-sounding name, but perhaps it's because so many people *see* sex as crude and rude. Nevertheless, dildos can be

a wonderful adjunct to lovemaking, allowing your man a breather
or picking up where he lets off after coming when you're wanting
more. Dildos are also wonderful after a self-induced orgasm. While
some women claim to be too sensitive after climaxing, I love to feel
a nice hard phallic-shaped object inside afterward.

I didn't discover the joys of dildos until one fateful opportunity
several years ago, when I was already in my thirties. I was attending one of my first AASECT (American Association of Sex Educators, Counselors, and Therapists) conferences where I was giving a
talk, and paid a visit to the exhibit hall where all sorts of sex
books, toys, and how-to videos for use in sexual counseling were
on display. At one table my eye was caught by a rather unusual-
looking phallus. It was made of strong black rubber and it was
large and shaped like a big penis with a handle resembling that of
a sword or a sheath. I was immediately drawn to it, as it appealed
to the side of me that likes things naughty and nasty. These products were not for sale, but rather just to show what was available
from that particular company, and there was a glass bowl for business cards, so I put one of mine in. About two weeks later I received a call from someone at the company informing me that they
had held a drawing and my card had been selected as one of the
winners and what would I like to have from their catalog? Well,
despite some of their other more elaborate and higher-priced
items, I didn't have to think twice about what I wanted. "The big
black rubber sheath dildo, please." Let me tell you, that nasty-
looking phallus has gotten a lot of use over the years. It's a bit
much for when I'm alone as I need to be very wet and loosened up
to accommodate it, but it sure is fun for partner play.

Dildos come in an endless variety of shapes and sizes and colors, from flesh-colored realistic with veins running up and down
the sides to smooth and candy colored. Some come in rubber,
some are made out of a soft material made to imitate the feeling of
flesh, and still others are made of silicone. Jamye tells me that sili-

cone dildos are best because you can boil them for three or four minutes to clean them. But she cautions not to use a silicone-based lube with silicone toys because the silicone of the lube will destroy the dildo. I'm also told that women are advised these days to use condoms on dildos and anything made with rubber because, while there's nothing definite known yet, there's some concern that the materials used to make rubber dildos may have potentially harmful effects on the user. In fact, it's probably just good basic advice to use condoms on any toy or vibe you might insert into the vagina.

Then you have Lucite toys that look more like an art object or are curved to hit the G-spot. Sources tell me that glass dildos are all the rage because you can cool them or heat them to make them more sanitary. Some of them are quite beautiful, but be fore-warned, they can be very pricey.

There's no end to the varieties and possibilities when it comes to dildos. A visit to your local sex shop or woman-friendly erotic emporium or a search on the Web will present you with a whole host of possibilities.

And finally, for those who are interested in exploring anal play, there's the butt plug. These are very handy because if you *are* going to insert something into your anus you *must* use something that has a handle or a flange that prevents the object from slipping up inside and getting lost inside your rectum. You don't want a fun night of sex adventure to end up in the emergency room with a doctor try-ing to remove something from inside your butt. As silly a name as "butt plug" may be, you'd be wise to use one if you want to feel the pleasurable sensations of anal play. They are also a good way to prep yourself if you're going to try anal sex with a partner. I'll delve into the—pardon the pun—ins and outs of anal sex in a later chap-ter as well as list some good books and videos in my resources list. In the meantime, it's important to sufficiently prepare yourself for anal intercourse and butt plugs are a great way to do it.

Now that you've got your vibrators and dildos picked out, let's move on to some other choice items to spice up your toy box.

Miscellaneous Toys and Accoutrements

Being creative and willing to play and try new things is essential if you want to keep your sex life interesting and exciting. One sure way to do that is to be willing to try out new and different playthings and games. I've already talked about bondage play and the thrill of surrender. If you share my curiosity for such occasional games, there are plenty of items to include in your toy box. To begin with, an assortment of silk or nylon scarves can be put to a variety of uses such as a blindfold or a restraint for tying the wrists together or to the bedposts—and remember, *you* can be the one tying *him* to the bedpost too! And speaking of blindfolds, those ordinary eye masks that airlines give out work like a charm. Of course erotic emporiums also carry sexy versions of the same in black, midnight blue, and who knows what other colors. In fact, bondage play has become so mainstream that one no longer has to go into those intimidating sex shops with studded leather masks that resemble the kind Hannibal Lechter wore alongside equipment straight out of some medieval torture chamber—that is, unless you *want* to. In the words of the late, great John Lennon, "Whatever gets you through the night." Like I said, just be sure you *both* know what you're doing and especially, that you *know him* very well.

There are all sorts of fun toys and equipment easily available now for bondage play, including various kinds of restraints—from your sweet safe satin or faux fur cuffs that close with easy "break-free" Velcro to the more serious leather cuffs and standard police-issue handcuffs for those sexy state trooper fantasy games—just don't lose the keys! There's literally something for everyone. My man happens to be a fervent lover of animals and refuses to eat or wear anything containing or made of animal products, including leather. Much to my delight he surprised me one day with a unique set of restraints that are made completely of synthetic materials with Velcro closures. "I looked a long time for something that wasn't made of leather," he confessed. Needless to say I was the happy recipient of his successful search.

For spanking enthusiasts, there is a wide array of paddles and other devices for corporal punishment, but a simple hairbrush reminiscent of the old spanking days could always suffice. A friend of mine even just started a Web site, spankingcream.com, for his Honey Bun collection of specialty creams and lotions to soothe the well-spanked buns.

For the more serious players, there are all kinds of riding crops, cat-o'-nine-tails, and whips, from the lightweight nylon variety to the hard-core leather. Again, not to overstate it, but just be sure you know what you're doing and whom you're doing it with.

Returning to the more benign play toys, there are also vibrating eggs to stimulate the inside of the vagina, and those sexy new remote-control vibrating panties. Eating out in a restaurant will never be the same!

For the more frivolous and playful approach, there are a host of new board games for lovers that can you give all sorts of new ideas to spice up the evening. These tend to be found more in women-friendly erotic stores and Web sites, which I include in my source list.

Slither Your Way to Safety: Lubes and Condoms

Every modern-day woman must have lubes and condoms in her toy box. Lubrication simply makes sex more slippery, wet, and therefore, more fun. It can enhance your lovemaking, prolong your pleasure, and give you endless satisfaction as you and your lover slither around each other. Condoms, however, are meant for safety. For those of you in long-term committed relationships, you may not need to use a condom—except for contraception. But for those of you who have not yet exchanged clean bills of health, indicating that both you and your lover are free of any sexually transmitted disease (STDs), then you should always use a condom when making love.

Lubes

There seems to be an infinite number of lubes to choose from on the market, but the type that's fast becoming a favorite among women is the silicone-based lube because of its ability to stay slippery for a *very* long time. Because it is not water based, and does not get absorbed into the skin or mucous membranes, it basically sits on top of the membranes or skin and *stays* slippery. But be careful because it's hard to wash off and if used in the bathtub or around other slippery surfaces can be a bit hazardous. It is condom safe and apparently the only products it doesn't do well with are other products made of silicone, including some dildos. The two most well known brands are I.D. lube and Eros.

Water-based lubes are also very popular and some are starting to add ingredients like arginine, which increases sensitivity and is good for both erectile function and for women who need a little help in getting stimulated. Be careful of water-based lubes that contain glycerin. Sex educator Jamye Waxman says that glycerin is actually a sugar and can lead to yeast infections in women who are prone to them.

Another ingredient you might avoid is nonoxynol-9, a spermicide. Nonoxynol-9 is a detergent and can cause irritation of the vaginal lining in some women. In fact, according to my sources, there is some concern that because it can create and lead to the opening up of irritated tissue, it can actually help spread the HIV virus.

If water-based lubes work for you, there are many popular

brands to choose from, including Slippery Stuff, Astroglide, Liquid Silk, and Maximus, which is thicker, making it good for vaginal and especially anal penetration. Jamye's two favorites are Sensual Power and Hydra Smooth because of their smooth texture and the fact that they have no taste.

DIRECTOR'S NOTE

You can easily reactivate water-based lubes during sex with a few drops of water.

Condoms

Long gone are the days when women relied on guys to pull out one of those old packs of condoms that look like they've been in a wallet for years while the guy was hoping to get lucky. Today's sexually active woman takes charge of her own sexual health and makes *sure* she has what she needs—should *she* get lucky. And don't fall for the old "you don't have to worry about me" line as he tries to squirm out of using one. You'd better worry about someone like him. Who knows how many *other* women to whom he's tried to sell that line? Remember: until you see a clean bill of health from a physician, *be safe*.

I knew times had changed when I began seeing cute and stylish little condom cases for women some years ago. Now what shall we put in them? Any visit to your local pharmacy should clue you in to what guys have had to face for years now: endless varieties and not a clue of which to pick. They even have stores just for condoms now, like New York City's Condomania, and Web sites too.

There are four types of condoms:

1. Latex, the most popular (make sure you read the ingredients of lubes and be sure they say "latex condom friendly").
2. Avanti, made of polyurethane, which is a strong thin material

that conducts heat, and is a good alternative for people who are allergic to latex.

3. Lamb's skin, the old-fashioned kind of condom, which I find kind of smelly; also, the thought of using lamb's skin is a bit of a turnoff to me—but that's just me. Far more important is the fact that lamb's skin is porous and therefore does not offer enough protection against the spread of the HIV virus or other STDs.

4. And just when you thought you knew everything you had to about condoms, they now have the female condom known as the Reality Condom. This new kind of condom is a soft, loose-fitting polyurethane sheath that lines the vagina. It has a soft ring at each end, one to help insert it, kind of like inserting a diaphragm, and the other to hold it in place during sex. That end stays outside the vagina, partially covering the labia, which is good for protecting you from contracting any sort of STD, but on the downside, it also doesn't look particularly attractive. It's also heavily lubed, and my source wasn't sure with what. Some women really like it and it's certainly effective.

There are condoms that are lubricated, but *what* are they lubricated *with?* Opt for condoms without lube in them and instead apply lube onto the man's cock before putting the condom on, thus enhancing his pleasure while penetrating you. Just be careful that the lube doesn't cause the condom to slide off during sex, something to be careful of in any case, especially if you go at it for a long time. I can recall the horror I once felt when I was using a condom to guard against pregnancy during my high-risk time of the month and my boyfriend basically fucked his way right through the condom! Fortunately nothing happened but it was a real wake-up call as to how fragile condoms can be. And as with lubes, stay away from condoms that contain nonoxynol-9.

There are also different-*sized* condoms. There's the Mamba, a smaller, tighter-fitting condom that might help solve the problem of it sliding off during sex. And there are the large-sized condoms like Magnum, Beyond 7 (self-explanatory), and Okeido, which is even longer. But be careful. I remember one time opening up the little condom box near my bed and realizing I was about to hand a large-sized condom to a lover with a somewhat small member. Thank Goddess I realized it before what could have been a terribly awkward moment for both of us.

Finally, there are all kinds of colored condoms, even ones that glow in the dark. I always liked black latex condoms 'cause I found them kind of nasty. The film director Veronica Hart shows a woman putting a black condom on her partner in one of my Femme movies, *Taste of Ambrosia*, in an effort to show condom use as unobtrusive to sex and even kind of sexy. Jamye Waxman says she doesn't feel the kind that are ribbed really do much for women, and that her favorite is the Crown brand, which are thin and pink.

Here's a funny story that highlights men's fragile egos: several years ago I was about to have sex for the first time with someone I had dated a few times. Thinking it was a funny sight, I showed him this huge box of candy-colored condoms someone had sent me, far more condoms than I could ever hope to go through before their expiration date! Well, our sex turned out less than stellar, in fact a dismal failure. He basically came as soon as he entered me and did that *all three times* he attempted to make love to me that night. Worse, he didn't even offer to help me get off in any other way and tried to act like nothing was wrong. Needless to say I *never* went out with *him* again! But sometime later I was told by a friend who introduced us that this guy had told him that he was totally freaked out by my showing him this huge box of condoms. I guess he missed the point of what was supposed to be funny, not a sign of my amazing number of sex partners. My hunch, however, is that this guy had some serious performance anxiety in the first place. But I would still caution you to take into account the fragile male ego when it comes to sex. Better to have a little box of two or three condoms at a time next to your bed rather than a drawer full of hundreds.

DIRECTOR'S NOTE

Be sure you know the proper way to put on a condom. There's a little pouch at the very tip of the condom meant to catch and contain the man's ejaculate. If this pouch is filled with air when it's on, it can be forced open by the ejaculation, rendering it ineffective. It's important that this little pouch be squeezed tight so there's no air in it when it's put on the guy's cock. Then you carefully roll down the rest of the condom on to the shaft of the already-erect penis. While many of us may rely on the guy to do the deed, there's nothing sexier for a guy than having the woman put the condom on for him. It becomes part of the sex play! So read a book, watch a video that teaches the right way to do it, ask a friend to show you. Do whatever you have to in order to learn, and then practice on a zucchini or a cucumber or something phallic shaped. It's a good skill to have. Besides, this way you'll *know* it's on right.

Are You Ready?

So what about *your* toy box? I would suggest taking a regular inventory just like any good production person to make sure your equipment is in good shape and ready to go. Here's a brief checklist to use as a review:

1. What's in your toy box?
2. Is it up to date?
3. Do you have the kinds of toys that you like and that get you off? Or is it time to look into some new ones?
4. Are your toys clean and ready to use?

5. Are the batteries in your vibrators still good?
6. Are your condoms still within their expiration date?
7. Is your jar or container of lube sticky and ready to be replaced? Is it latex safe if you're planning on using condoms?
8. Is there something you've been wanting to purchase or try that would make for an interesting addition?
9. Is there something special that your man would like that you might surprise him with?

Remember, toys that are old or appear to be unclean can be a real turnoff to a lover. Same goes for sticky, messy lube jars. How would *you* feel if a new paramour had you over to his place and pulled something out of his stash to use on you that appeared to be old, worn out, unclean, and, worse, used on someone before you? We may not be the first one he used those Velcro cuffs on but we at least would like to *think* we are. Same goes for him. We all know others came before us but no one wants to be reminded when we're in the throes of passion. And, equally important, how we maintain our personal intimate items reflects how we take care of ourselves. Just as we take great pains to be clean and fresh smelling in preparation for good lovemaking, we should also make sure our equipment is clean and fresh and ready to go.

Now that you're outfitted with the best toy box full of all your clean and working equipment, let's move on to prepping the leading actress—*you*. In the next chapter you will get ready—from head to toe—by preparing your own very special boudoir.

Chapter 8

The Boudoir Ritual

A beautiful girl is an accident. A beautiful woman is a
creation of her own self.
—ancient Chinese proverb

Start the Cameras Rolling

O ne of my favorite things to do before a special night of lovemaking is to prepare myself with what I call my "beauty
bath." I revel in this ritual—the bath, the oils and creams,
selecting my outfit and what goes underneath, choosing the scent
I'm in the mood for that night. Taking this time to prepare literally
becomes a part of the foreplay for me. As I bathe and dress, I am
imagining what might happen that night. This chapter is filled
with ideas to inspire your own sensual treat, one that relaxes you
and arouses you. Certainly one woman's personal beauty ritual
might seem like another's burden; we all have our own ideas of
what we like or are willing to do. Whether you're a nature girl who
prefers to go au naturel and forego any makeup or perfumes, pre-
ferring to take a run, spin class, or yoga as a way to prep for your
hot date, or you are more of a "painted woman," who revels in all
the best beauty products on the market, I urge you to indulge in

some serious pampering before a special date. It can make you feel beautiful and confident and ready for romance. You'll also feel and smell wonderful to your lover.

If the ritual I describe here doesn't strike your fancy, I encourage you to create one of your very own. One woman told me she prepares for dates by working out: she loves to run three miles, lift light free weights, and then take a lukewarm shower. Why? As she said, "I love to get my blood pumping—I feel invigorated and sexy." As I always tell women, we don't have to have perfect bodies to be lovable and desirable. Just have the right lighting, enhance your body with the right clothes or lingerie, have soft fragrant skin that smells wonderful, a pussy that tastes delicious, and your man will become intoxicated with you!

YOU ARE WHAT YOU EAT

Here are some tips on how to naturally smell and taste wonderful, as well as things to avoid. For fragrant skin and a good tasting pussy:

1. Eat a diet rich in fruits and vegetables.
2. Drink lots of water; water is a natural cleanser, removing toxins that build up in the body. It also hydrates the skin from the inside out.
3. Avoid heavy amounts of alcohol. It comes out through the pores, creating a sour smell as well as a sour-tasting pussy.
4. Avoid eating lots of meat and animal products. The cleaner and freer of animal products your diet is, the better you'll smell and taste.

The Beauty Ritual

So, how do we achieve this intoxicating state? It's time for our beauty ritual.

Prepare Your Bath

Begin by choosing either a scented oil, one that will lightly moisturize and coat your skin with a subtle layer of smooth rich oil, or a fragrant bath salt that invigorates and softens your skin. Pay attention to the particular herbs that are used. Citrus scents tend to be invigorating, while lavender and ylang-ylang are relaxing and sensual. There are many wonderful bath products on the market, far too many not to indulge in. Read the labels, as good bath salts and oils will list the properties of their ingredients, like the ones above, and what you can expect from them.

Nail Care for Ladies Who Love

Next see whether you need to attend to either your fingernails or your toenails. Treat yourself to a manicure/pedicure at your favorite salon. If you're between appointments, or don't have the time earlier that day, check to see if your nails need any filing or primping. I tend to leave my fingernails natural now. After twenty years of wearing colored nail polish, my nails rebelled and refused to grow. What I happily discovered was that leaving my fingernails natural actually makes the fingers look longer and more tapered. My nails grew back long and strong, and I've discovered that if you ask the manicurist to simply buff your nails they come out looking smooth and shiny without the use of abrasive products.

Some men actually prefer the natural look. I'll never forget one ex-beau who laughed when he saw my toes and remarked that they looked like Chiclets! And after all that trouble I went to for him. Have your feet and hands and toe- and fingernails as ready as every other part of your body. How we tend to such personal details says a lot about what we think of ourselves. Besides, you never know when you're going to get one of the many men who adore women's feet. And if you are with such a man, there's nothing like having him tenderly paint your toenails *for* you. Yum!

Pussy Pampering

Finally, before stepping into your bath, tend to perhaps the most personal aspect of your beauty ritual, especially if you're expecting—or hoping—to make love that night. Tend to your pussy. Does it need a little trim? Do you want to neaten up your bikini line? Even if you're not sure if the evening's definitely going to end up between the sheets, it's good to know that you're completely ready and feeling comfortable with what's going on down there.

Each woman has a different vision of how she likes her pubic mound to look. For me it's a neat trim and then a bit of a shave in the tub around my bikini line. Some women like to go all out, and get what's become known as a "Brazilian." This type of pubic wax is done by a professional at a salon and entails waxing and then removing all of the hair around your genitals—up, down, and under. They do protect the tender mucous membranes and other terribly sensitive areas, but otherwise, this form of wax is fairly drastic. I personally find this style a bit excessive, but we all have our levels of what we're wanting or willing to do. I used to get my bikini line waxed at Elizabeth Arden in New York, one of the best places you can go to have it done, and it was so painful that I can only imagine what it feels like to do the entire genital area. Not to mention that waxing can cause lots of unsightly ingrown hairs, plus you have to let it grow out a bit to be able to do it again.

And keep in mind that some men love a healthy bush on a woman. So if you're with such a man, consider yourself lucky and ignore the whole issue. But for those of you looking for the best way to remove your pubic hairs, here are some tips:

○ The best thing to use for shaving bikini lines as well as genitalia, if you're going that route, is—believe it or not—hair conditioner. Porn stars swear by it, and sure enough, they're absolutely right. It seems the oils in the conditioner tend to protect the skin and provide for a close shave without irritation. I have discovered a product called—are you ready?—COOCHY Rash Free Body Shave Cream (made by Holiday Products in Canoga Park, California). It's got jojoba oil and lanolin in it, two of the best ingredients for hair and skin products. It stands to reason someone would think to take what's in hair conditioner and market it that way. One word of caution: if you *are* going to shave all the hair off your genitals, be forewarned that things get awfully irritated down there once the hair starts growing back in. You can develop a really itchy rash.

○ If you are going to use a depilatory cream, use it at least twenty-four hours in advance. Most of these creams smell pretty weird and the smell tends to take a good twenty-four hours to dissipate. But they do leave you feeling very smooth and the hair doesn't start to grow back for at least a few days.

THE ART OF PUSSY TRIMMING—FOR HIM

I once wrote an article called "The Art of Pussy Trimming." It advised men that if they learned how to artfully trim their lover's pussy they would become a better lover. The point was that if a man was willing to take the time and patience required to trim his woman's pussy hair, it would teach him patience and delicacy of touch as a lover. I learned this from a ritual my ex-husband and I had created, whereby I would lay down on a towel on the bed and he would gently and gingerly give me a long, slow pussy trim. I can tell you that the other benefit to this boudoir ritual was that being so teasingly touched for so long was wonderful foreplay. Inevitably it led us to hot, hot sex, right then and there. I took this unique form of foreplay a step further with my next lover and learned to trim his pubes as well. What fun that was to see his member become more and more uncontrollably engorged with each delicate touch of my hands. Of course we must also be very careful with those sharp instruments down there. One slip of the hand and it may be the last time he lets you down there!

Relax in a Luxurious Bath

Now that you've got your nails checked and your pubes trimmed and ready, it's time to light a candle, light some incense if you're so inclined, select some relaxing music, and sink into your hot, waiting bath. Mmmmmm, it makes me want to go draw a bath right now! I usually allow myself some time to relax and luxuriate in the hot steamy salts and oils for a bit, letting my thoughts drift off and my mind calm. I also like to do this ritual just for meditative thinking, especially if I have something on my mind I need to think about and resolve. We can have some wonderful thoughts and ideas in this state. Knowing we have a special erotic evening ahead makes this phase only more delicious as we anticipate what might take place. I sometimes can't resist pleasuring myself while in such a state. You may want to keep your little waterproof vibe on hand for such opportunities.

Relish the Water

After a bit of a soak in the oil-scented water, your skin needs some more attention. First, take a loofah, and scrub your skin all over, not too hard, just enough to remove the dead skin cells. (Loofahs grow naturally in the sea and, while they feel hard and scratchy when dry, they soften up once they're wet. You can find good loofahs in most health food stores and natural beauty products shops.) This exfoliation is the best way to keep your skin soft and youthful. It sloughs off the top layer of dead cells and invigorates and promotes the regeneration of new skin, leaving you feeling more supple and smooth. I guarantee you that this combined with a good quality body cream will give you the softest skin imaginable.

After scrubbing your entire body with your loofah, including your back, it's time to do your feet, whether it's with an old-fashioned pumice stone or one of the newer hand-held foot scrubbers. There's nothing more unattractive on a woman's feet than thick calluses from all the bad shoes we wear. It's easy to keep these at bay if you do this regularly.

Next comes the shaving of legs and wherever else you choose to shave.

And finally it's time to wash. Never apply soap on the skin of your legs and arms and mid-area, since soap can be very drying. It's better to loofah this skin instead. Only use soap on your anal area, under your arms, and on your genitals. And even on my genitals I sometimes prefer to use a special low-pH soap to prevent irritation of the mucous membranes. There are at least two soaps on the market specific to this, including one called Delicate from my own Natural Contours line.

SOAPS BEWARE

Soaps can be very drying and irritating. The more they suds up, the worse they are for you. Most commercial-brand soaps are far too hard on our skin, full of harsh detergents, synthetic fragrances, dyes, and animal products. I use soaps from health food stores that are rich in oils and have a low pH, making them less drying to the skin. The lower the pH content, the less it will suds up, but that doesn't mean it isn't cleaning you. Look for soaps made up of natural vegetable oils and without sodium lauryl or laureth sulfate (detergents), like the Avalon Organic Botanicals line.

Rinse

Now you're clean, smooth, and hairless where you want to be, but your bathwater is pretty grimy, so it's time to stand up, rinse off in a nice hot shower, and wash and condition your hair. I always choose products with ingredients that are natural and cruelty free, meaning there are no harsh chemicals in them, they're friendly to the environment, they do not contain any animal products, and there's no animal testing conducted in the making of this product.

Today we have plenty of proven data available so that brutal cosmetic testing is absolutely unnecessary, and herbal ingredients are just as good and easily affordable so that we no longer need to use animal ingredients for superior quality makeup and cosmetics. When it comes to shampoo and conditioner, choose the most natural products while still getting your hair clean.

It's becoming a popular new trend in some hair circles to discourage people from shampooing so frequently and with such harsh cleansers. We're taught how awful it is to have oily skin and hair. Now I know that I'm actually quite fortunate to have been born with oil-rich skin and hair. The more oil we have in our skin, the less it will wrinkle and dry as we age. And the more oil we have in our hair the more lustrous it will remain. Be careful of harsh hair products. Because my cells regenerate more quickly than the average person, it also sloughs off more quickly, creating the appearance of dandruff. I opt for more natural medicated shampoos that I find in health food stores because, as a pharmacist once explained to me, the commercial brand dandruff shampoos work by harshly removing the entire top layer of cells all at once. But all this does is make the scalp reproduce cells all the more quickly, forcing you to search out ever more harsh products. Same with overwashing—the more often you wash your hair the more quickly it produces oils to compensate. Great for the shampoo industry! I wash my hair every three days now, and when I can, I'll even go an extra day as a sort of special treatment, brushing the oils down to the ends of my hair to bathe them in this natural nourishing richness. Another tip: if you have long hair, put conditioner on the ends before you shampoo the roots. And never apply shampoo directly onto the ends.

Be careful also about hair color products. I have my hair color-treated with the most natural of products used at my salon, avoiding unnecessary damage to the hair. You might want to search for a salon that goes the extra mile to search out gentle products. The brand they use is Schwarzkopf and what makes it so much less abrasive to the hair is its low ammonia content.

DIRECTOR'S NOTE

A special note for all you women with natural curls: one of the owners of the Devachan Salon and Spa in Manhattan, where I get my hair done, has written a wonderful book especially for you. It's called *Curly Girl: The Handbook,* by Lorraine Massey, and it's all about how to best care for your natural curls and embrace your inner curly girl. I would urge any of you who would like to stop torturing your hair in order to make it straight to get that book. We women always want what we don't have. When I was a little girl I always wanted curly hair. My hair was so defiantly straight that even the permanent waves my mother painstakingly attempted to put in my hair wouldn't take. I eventually came to appreciate my straight hair and I would urge all of you curly girls to indulge in your goddesslike curly locks.

DIRECTOR'S NOTE

Tips on Healthy Hair, Skin, and Use of Products

- Wash your hair less often.
- Put conditioner on the ends of long hair while washing the scalp.
- Never apply shampoo to the ends of hair.
- Seek out a salon that uses hair color and dyes with the lowest ammonia content.
- Use low-pH content soaps and shampoos to avoid drying.
- Seek out an extra-low-pH soap for the vagina so as not to irritate the delicate mucous membranes.
- Seek out natural products that use herbs and natural vegetable oils, and avoid sodium lauryl and laureth sulfate.
- Try to use products that are cruelty free so as to not support unnecessary harm to our animal friends.
- Use soap only on your anal area, genitals, feet, and underarms.

○ Loofah outer extremities to remove dead cells and stimulate new
skin growth.

○ Apply a natural hydrating cream to your entire body after the
bath.

Final Touches

By the time you step out of the bath, you should be feeling delicious, ever closer to your night of seduction. Next it's time to
brush your teeth and finish cleansing and moisturizing your face,
again with gentle but stimulating, cruelty-free products. The final
and equally important step is to rub cream into your entire body. I
actually do this every time I step out of a bath or shower. The older
we get the more our skin suffers from the elements and ravages of
time. I believe this ritual of creaming my skin every time I bathe
along with the regular loofah cleansing (which I do not actually do
every day) has really been effective. I must tell you that the older
I've gotten, the more I've had men marveling over how soft my
skin is. I've had my skin likened to that of a baby's butt. Now,
that's rewarding!

CREAMS AND LOTIONS

I sometimes use peppermint-infused cream on my feet,
which helps them stay fresh and clean. As for body creams, I
again opt for the natural ingredients and I completely stay away
from anything with mineral oil, as it clogs the pores and feels
greasy. If your skin gets particularly dry, and during those winter
months when the air is quite dry, you might try using a hydrating cream, which means it's extra rich and absorbent. Lotions
are the thinnest and least effective. Some of my favorite brands
are Kiss My Face, which makes wonderful creams for the body,
and Beauty Without Cruelty, Jason Cosmetics, and Orgene for

facial products, again found at most health food stores. And for those of you willing to spend a little more, my beau turned me on to a wonderful line of ultranatural products called Jurlique. If your guy's as sweet as mine, maybe you can even get him to buy some for you!

ALUMINUM BEWARE

While I'm on the subject of natural products, be good to yourself and stop using deodorants that contain aluminum, also sometimes called alum, aluminum chlorohydrate, or aluminum chlorohydroxide. Aluminum is absorbed into the body and some studies show it plays a role in the development of Alzheimer's disease. If you can't find any deodorants without aluminum in your drugstore, health food stores have many good natural deodorants.

DIRECTOR'S NOTE

A note about antiperspirants: antiperspirant deodorants clog the pores under the arms. Since sweating is nature's way of getting rid of toxins in the body (as well as cooling your body), blocking your pores can cause toxins to build up in the lymph nodes under the arm. There is growing concern that this might contribute to breast cancer. Your safest bet is to stay clean and fresh-smelling by bathing daily (with nonabrasive soaps, of course!) and eating as clean and pure a diet as possible. Then opt for the many available natural, aluminum-free deodorants currently on the market.

Applying body cream feels like a wonderful ritual of self-love. To spend so much time sensuously massaging creams into your skin keeps you in touch with your body and your delight in being touched. I recall some years ago after a particularly hard breakup, I knew that while I was going to really miss being touched so sensuously, I wanted to also spend some time alone without jumping into bed with anyone for a while. So I began getting regular massages to make sure I continued being touched, something I feel is so important to our well-being. And don't leave out your breasts. Stimulating the breast tissue is healthy and important. There was a study some years ago that encouraged men to massage and rub their wives' breasts because it helped guard against the growth of tumors. I remember thinking, *Well, I massage my breasts every day when I put cream on them.* Of course the idea of a woman doing that to *herself* was still considered too racy to promote, or maybe too self-empowering. Though I admit, it's lots more fun to have our guy do it for us!

Hair and Makeup

Now it's time to do your hair and makeup. Using a rounded brush with your blow dryer is far less drying and damaging to the hair than using a curling iron. There are also lots of good products to help hold in style and prevent flyaway hair, but if you're like me and have plenty of natural oils in your hair, you may not need any of these. Because I don't want to have to redo my hair every day, I avoid adding gels and creams to my hair because they make it get oily that much faster. A little tip I learned from a hair and makeup artist: occasionally rinsing your hair with a simple solution of baking soda mixed with water helps remove the buildup on our scalp from hair products.

DIRECTOR'S NOTE

While heavy red lips might be suitable for certain situations, I've moved on to a more natural look of tinted lips. I often blend different shades of lip color to get exactly what I want. For those who, like myself, prefer cosmetics that use more natural ingredients, I've found a wonderful line called Alba Terra Tints, also sometimes la-

beled as Avalon Un-Petroleum. The lipsticks come in lots of wonderful tints that I sometimes mix and match, and are made with terrific
ingredients that don't harm you or your animal friends!

DIRECTOR'S NOTE

Baking soda provides several ways to give you an easy, inexpen-
sive beauty treatment.

- For a gently invigorating facial scrub, mix three parts baking soda
  with one part water to form a thick paste; apply in a gentle circular motion. This also makes a great smoother for skin on feet and
  heels.
- For smooth skin all over, add one-half cup baking soda to a warm
  bath. Baking soda naturally cleanses your skin and its white crystals are often a key ingredient in commercial bath salts. If your
  skin is dry, be sure to rinse well, as an alkaline residue may irritate the skin.
- For cleansing the scalp, remove residue that hair styling products
  and shampoos might leave behind by adding baking soda (about
  the size of a quarter) to your shampoo. Rinse and condition as
  usual.
- For extra-clean combs and brushes, fill your basin with a quart of
  water and dissolve four tablespoons of baking soda in the water.
  Soak combs and brushes for a few minutes, then swish, rinse, and
  air dry.

This information is courtesy of *Prevention* magazine.

As for makeup, it's best to go simple and natural. I'm always
amazed by how many of my men prefer me in as little makeup as
possible, especially foundation, which can actually make you look
older when it's applied too heavily! The secret is to learn how to
apply makeup in such a way that makes it appear as if you're not
wearing any. I've been fortunate that for so many years I've had
professionals do my makeup for TV and film appearances. I always
pay attention to what they do. But if you're not privy to such pam-

pering, try going to your local department store where they often have professionals who will show you how to apply your makeup for free, in exchange for trying to sell you products. And again, no need to buy products that still unnecessarily test on animals or even use animal ingredients. The more natural the better it is for your skin anyway. There are a growing number of brands that are adopting a "cruelty-free" policy, including the popular M.A.C. and Aveda product lines. It will state on the label if they are cruelty free and you can also write them or ask them point blank if they have adopted this policy.

One last note about your beauty ritual: there's nothing worse than a woman who wears too much perfume! A light misting of perfume on the neck and between the breasts, maybe a dab between thighs—but not on the labia, it doesn't necessarily taste good—is ample. I reserve the privilege of breathing in my scents for just that one lucky man. I always love when my man leans in close to my neck and discovers with delight that I've put on just a dash of scent for his nose only. And I always stay true to just one or two scents that come to identify me to him. Whenever he smells those aromatic fragrances he will forever think of me.

The best way to apply perfume:

○ Spray it into the air and walk through the mist, so that it falls lightly upon you.
○ Very lightly spray or dab a tiny extra bit of it on your neck, and wherever else you like to secretly place it for your lover to discover. Just remember, do so sparingly. You want your lover to discover it, not be smothered in it. Men still prefer the natural scents of a woman. A hint of perfume is meant to simply enhance your own personal scent, not cover it.

Now put on that outfit and get ready for your close-up. It's time to call *action* and bring your private movie to life!

Phase Three

The Shoot, or Action!

Chapter 9

Rehearse Your Lines

Sex is a conversation carried out by other means.
—Peter Ustinov, interview with Wendy Leigh, *Speaking Frankly*

ommunicating sexual desire is a very subtle art, and yet it is a
pillar of great sex. Being receptive to and *remembering* what
your lover communicates to you is equally important. One of
the greatest compliments a lover ever gave me was that I was sensitive—to his needs, to his feelings, to his touch. He said that I
paid attention to what he liked and wanted. But he also said how
powerful it was for him that I responded to everything he did to
me, every touch, with every part of my body. Being able to pay attention and respond was what in his eyes made me a wonderful
lover. I never forgot this experience and it remains for me a measure of whether someone is indeed a good lover or not.

A good lover must be able to communicate her desires to her
partner. She must also be able to listen to his desires, be willing to
compromise, and be attuned to his cues. Sex, like a good film production, requires sensitive and subtle communication between all

those involved. As director, I have to be a clear communicator of what I want to happen, but I also must give my actors enough freedom to interpret and act from an authentic place, one that is comfortable for them and makes them want to respond. Creating this harmony requires that I be both strong and sensitive. This is also true when you are directing your own passionate production with your man: you must be able to communicate your desires clearly but you also must pay attention to his responses. If you want him to continue pleasuring you with his fingers before he begins to enter you, then let him know what a master he is. If you begin to investigate his body, does he relax or contract as you head toward his butt?

As crucial to great sex as communication is, it also happens to be one of the most difficult skills to master. I'd like to take a little time here to focus on why and how we can improve our communication skills. For without them, all the greatest plans and bedroom scripts will go nowhere if we don't know how to direct them.

The Good Girl—Bad Girl Myth

As I mentioned in the introduction to this book, I believe for women the biggest barrier to communicating our needs goes back to the age-old good girl–bad girl stigma and the double standard that says it's OK for young men to sexually experiment before marriage but not young women. As much as we may believe we're way beyond those hang-ups, exorcizing such long imbedded mores takes a long time, far more than one generation of bra-burning feminists. I myself was stunned to realize just how insecure I felt about asking for what I need. It was several years ago when I had taken up with a new guy. I really liked him, hot looking, sexy, successful—only problem was he didn't make love to me the way I liked. I was telling a girlfriend about it and how I felt it probably wouldn't work out when she said very matter-of-factly, "Just tell him what you like." I was taken aback, both by the simplicity of what she was suggesting and at how insurmountable that felt to me. It made me realize just how inhibited I actually was, even after all the years I'd spent in relationships, not to mention the fact that I was considered something of a sex expert. I also thought, *If I feel this way, think how many other women must feel this way.*

Granted, there are those fortunate women who don't have this hang-up, especially today's younger women who have the benefit of their mothers' generation of feminists who began breaking through outmoded mores and claiming their right to good sex. I have a twenty-five-year-old cousin who tells me that the first thing she does with a new beau is instruct him in the fine art of how she likes to get head—just to "get that out of the way"! I admire her lack of inhibition and wish I could be the same way. But like so many, I still carry around a certain level of uncertainty fueled by yesterday's tired old messages about good girls versus bad girls, and it takes real conscious effort on my part to break through those inhibitions. But when I do, the rewards are worth it.

So just what's behind those old good girl–bad girl messages? Without going into a whole feminist diatribe of how women have been sexually repressed for a whole slew of reasons, it boils down to the fear that uncontrolled sex will turn us in to lawless pagans engaging in nonstop orgies. "Good women" are charged with keeping their oversexed men in line, forgiving their poor horny dogs an occasional dalliance with a "bad girl" for pay. This cultural premise also serves to address what I believe is a deep-rooted fear that the sexually empowered woman will leave her family and run wild in the streets like an out-of-control nymphomaniac. Put women in charge of our morality and condemn those who don't conform to these roles and you've got a twofold solution for the dangers of unbridled lust.

For so long we've been kept ignorant of our sexual powers and convinced that good women don't have the same sexual drive as men. Remember what the late Dr. Masters of Masters and Johnson said? That "women's capacity for pleasure would put any man to shame." In most cases my capacity for pleasure far surpassed the men I was with, including my serious relationships. For years I feared I would never get to experience the incredible pleasure I am capable of. I would have to admit that only twice in my adult life have I found men who were as sensual, as creative and fierce as I am in bed, and who could keep up with me. My friend Josephine Bouio describes it as "the curse of the sex goddess," and that's often how it felt. I'm very happy to say that the man I'm with now has allayed my fears and made me believe there *are* men out there who can match us. They may be few and far between, but they're out there.

But more important, we can make our man into the lover we want, or at least close to it. We just need to break through those unfair and restricting messages and learn how to convey our needs to him. I know now that when I feel reticent about asking for what I need, I'm afraid that he'll think I've had sexual experience, that I'm not an innocent, pure woman, that I'm a "bad girl." Add to that the fear of hurting his male ego by showing that he in fact doesn't necessarily know how my body works.

So where does that leave us when it comes to letting a man know what we actually need? It keeps us silent and unfulfilled as we lie there passively wishing he could read our thoughts. Which brings me to another important aspect of all this: how *can* a man know what we want right off the bat unless he's a mind reader? And what a burden for men to have to come off like the all-knowing Don Juan. How many times have we heard men complain that women expect them to read their minds when it comes to sex? So we're both victims of this cruel and outmoded double standard, yet we seem to hold on to it all the same.

With all these mixed messages about how women are supposed to behave, it's no wonder that we're still shy in bed and afraid to let on that we just might know a thing or two about our bodies and how to have great sex. The only way to combat this inhibiting mindset is to become consciously aware of what's behind our reticence and make up our minds that we are entitled to enjoy the wonderful pleasure we're capable of. And that regardless of what the culture still tries to tell us in a myriad of verbal and nonverbal ways, we are going to cast off these tired old messages and take what is rightfully ours. And that any man who can't accept that we are women who are in charge of our lives, our bodies, and our pleasure is not worth our time and effort. Besides, it's been my experience that men who need to feel like the knowledgeable experienced ones are covering up an underlying insecurity about themselves and their sexuality. I've found that the men who are the most giving and compassionate lovers are those who don't need to prop up their egos by feeling sexually superior to the woman they're with. My man loves that I am in touch with my sexuality and can give it as good as I get it. He knows that regardless of how many lovers I may have had, I'm now with the one I want to be with and for me he is the best.

CANDIDA'S CLOSE-UP

Q: I'm a male in my mid-fifties. My wife masturbates and loves performing the act while I masturbate to her masturbating . . . it's a wonderful experience. My question: why do so few videos have scenes that truly represent female masturbation in its glory? All the ladies seem to feel that the more noise, screaming, body movement, and exaggerating, the better. Fact is, I've seen a number of beautiful women masturbate while I masturbated with them. Not one screamed. Not one oohed, or cooed, or the rest of that jazz. Please, someone please, tell these gals to be natural.

A: I'm well aware of how erotic it can be to watch your lover masturbate. Not only do many men find it incredibly exciting to watch a woman pleasure herself, many women love watching men masturbate as well. Many of my movies feature women masturbating. I guess I not only find it exciting and beautiful to look at, I also think it's very healthy for women to masturbate. They learn about their bodies and what turns them on. This leads to more fulfilling sex lives with their partners. And I agree that to portray this in an obviously fake manner really takes away from the beauty and excitement. If you haven't seen any of my Femme films, I will tell you the ones I think have the best scenes of women masturbating. One is *The Gift*, starring Shanna McCullough, who not only performs beautifully, but claims to have really climaxed in this scene. Another stand-out is *Three Daughters*, which features a wonderful scene where the youngest daughter (she's of legal age!) learns how to have an orgasm by masturbating.

Saying It Out Loud

There will always be times when your lover just can't seem to do what you need to make you writhe in pleasure and scream out for more. So how do you solve the problem? You ask for what you want!

Unfortunately, this task can often feel uncomfortable for women—and men. Even the most seemingly confident men often display an amazing sensitivity when it comes to his image as a proficient lover. I can recall several years ago being rather shocked at a lover's response to my simple request to have him finger-fuck me while I played with my clitoris. It wasn't easy for me to ask in the first place, especially because I knew how much men liked to think that women will come endlessly by being fucked or having oral sex performed on them, and because I still had lingering feelings that my way of climaxing was "inferior." So, when I broached the subject, it felt awkward for me. But I took a deep breath and sweetly asked, "Honey, would you put your fingers inside me while I play with myself?" He did it, but rather begrudgingly, as he did the next few times as well. Finally, I asked him why, and he said, "Because I feel like it's not really me, you don't really need *me*." I was a bit shocked. Then I took a deep breath and explained to him that why it was so exciting for me was because it was *him* doing it. His holding me in his arms and doing this delicious thing to me was what got me all excited, and that what he was doing with his fingers inside of my vagina, massaging all those wonderful hidden-away areas including my G-spot, felt incredibly good and made my orgasms far more explosive than if I was doing it all by my lonesome. I also explained that just as his penis is attached to him, so is his tongue and so are his fingers.

He got it. And he became excellent at the art of internal vaginal massage and G-spot stimulation. I always felt like I should extract payment from the women who came after me for what a good G-spotter he became thanks to my tutelage.

So even though you may feel awkward or fearful detailing what you want your man to do for you, you must take the plunge and tell him.

There are two distinct times to tell your man how you prefer to be sexually pleasured: when it's happening and after the fact. It's often suggested that you withhold your discussions about what you like and don't like for outside the bedroom so you don't interrupt the flow or make your lover feel like he's got to perform to your requirements. I'll discuss in chapter 11 the process of recalling and reviewing what you liked and didn't like together, so for now let's focus on the far more delicate art of asking for specifics when in the throes of passion.

It's always best to lead off with what you *like*, or what you are enjoying at the moment. In other words, if you come out with something like, "ouch, that's not how I like it," you might interrupt an otherwise potentially great lovemaking session. You need to always tread lightly and err on the side of gentleness when it comes to offering sexual direction. After all, you're dealing with someone's need to feel like he can pleasure you. No one minds a little constructive criticism, but he doesn't want to feel like he's being judged and criticized by a drill sergeant. You would get a lot farther by saying something like, "Mmm, that feels nice, could you do that a little slower?" . . . or faster, or whatever it is you prefer.

It's still awkward the first time I want to show my man how I like to get off. I might start off by saying, "Mmm, you've got me so hot, I'd love to touch myself while you play with me," or, "It really turns me on to have your fingers inside of me while I play with myself." If a man has been trying to get me off by giving me oral sex, which usually doesn't get me all the way there, I might say to him, "You're really good at that. You've got me so close I'd love you to put your fingers in me while I play with myself." In other words, you're giving him positive reinforcement while at the same time letting him know exactly what you'd like next. He doesn't have to feel like he's done anything wrong or poorly while also learning that there's something else you need instead.

Since men are so acculturated to be the one who knows about sex, you'll get a lot more out of your lover if you learn to make him feel good about himself and his abilities as a lover—even when you need to teach him a whole new bag of tricks. We all want to feel like we know a thing or two about how to please someone and that our touch is magic to him.

Paying Attention to Him

The best way to know what your lover likes is to pay attention to his responses. Listen for the moans and groans, the "oh yeses" and watch for the undulating hips. But not everyone is sensitive enough to listen and pay attention as closely as she should and not every lover is demonstrative enough to let you know when he's really enjoying a particular move.

Don't assume that what works on one lover will automatically be what sends your next lover into heights of ecstasy. One of the most obvious examples of this is how you perform oral sex on a man. I had a lover who loved it when I was rough with him, even when it came to giving him head. He actually liked when I would lightly rake my teeth along the shaft of his cock, perhaps enjoying the sense of danger that gave him. Sometime later after we broke up and I was with my next lover I made the grave mistake of doing the same thing to him. Well, he almost whacked me! I've since learned that *most* men consider any kind of rough treatment of their penis to be painful, not pleasurable. Since then, I've never assumed that my new man might like what my last man liked.

I've also been asked many times over the years, "What's the best way to give a great blow job?" or "How can I be a great lover?" The best piece of advice I can give anyone is that the best way to do anything is to do it the way your lover likes. No two people are exactly alike. You would be wise to ask your lover what he likes and to pay attention to clues. I could give you all kinds of detailed tips, some of which might please your lover, some which might not, but the most important thing is to communicate with each other and find out specifically what *your* lover likes, not what someone else *thinks* he might like. Becoming intimate with someone requires time and sensitivity. We can't expect to enter into a new relationship and get it all right immediately. Part of the thrill is getting to know each other and what drives each of you to ecstatic heights. I've learned never to place much importance on the first time a new lover and I consummate our relationship, but rather to look forward to learning more about each other in what can potentially be a wonderful journey into our own garden of Eros.

ASKING YOUR MAN

Here are some tips on how to ask what he likes:

- ○ I love touching you. Do you like a gentle caress or do you like to be handled rough?
- ○ I'd love to give you head; how do you like it, fast or slow?
- ○ You have such a cute butt; do you enjoy anal play?
- ○ When I suck you, do you like me to use my hands as well as my mouth?
- ○ What's your favorite position?
- ○ Would you like to try it with me on top?

Introducing Toys and Allaying the Fragile Male Ego

One of the most commonly asked questions I get from women is how to introduce the use of vibrators and dildos to their partner without making him feel threatened. It would be easy for me to say, "Any man who's confident about his sexuality shouldn't feel threatened by the use of sex toys." However, just as when men are asked to do something differently, some men can feel awfully threatened by the introduction of something that isn't attached to his anatomy.

The experience of asking that new lover to use his fingers gave me good insight into the fragile male ego and their attachment to the almighty phallus as the premier provider of pleasure. Without pointing out the fallacy underlying such an assumption (considering how unreliable the penis can be), I will point out a couple of well-known facts: a penis often doesn't want to perform when women want or need it to, and all too often it's just a bit too quick on the trigger to satisfy the hours of enjoyment many women are capable of. (I always say *women* are the ones who should have harems!)

The solution to these precarious penis traits: sex toys. They are a great way to step in and supplement the degree of pleasure we can take, especially if the man is able to get it up again once he gets through his refractory period, the time it takes to relax and then get erect again.

DIRECTOR'S NOTE

It takes about twenty minutes for the average woman to be stimulated enough to climax—whether it's through direct clitoral stimulation or intercourse. At the same time, according to a remarkable study done by *Penthouse* magazine several years ago, the average amount of time a man has intercourse before coming is—are you ready?—two and a half minutes! Fortunately, many men as they grow older learn how to hold back and last far longer than that. But according to my informal survey, most men only last about ten minutes and think a twenty- to thirty-minute session of lovemaking is quite amazing. Not great for someone like me who loves to linger for at least an hour if not several when I truly adore someone!

So how do you introduce your man to the use of vibrators and dildos without making him feel inadequate or left out? First of all, bring it up as an idea for partner play. I recall telling a young filmmaker about my line of Natural Contours vibrators. He visited my Web site and e-mailed me saying, "Nice line Candida, but I guess there's nothing in it for me." "Au contraire," I replied. "Two can play as well as one!" In fact, I once had a boyfriend pull out one of my vibrators and begin using it on himself. So suggest it as a fun toy for *both* of you to play with, whether the idea is for him to use it on you, or, if he can handle the suggestion, to use it on himself—or, of course, for you to use it on him.

When suggesting that he pleasure you with a dildo or a vibrator, be clear that it's the fact that *he's* using it on *you*, or that he's there *with* you that makes it so exciting. Of course anyone would dislike the idea that he could slip away and you'd hardly notice because you're so busy with your sex toys, but if he feels like he's an integral part of it he shouldn't feel left out and threatened by the addition of this innocuous little toy.

Another suggestion is to find a dildo or vibe that matches the size of his penis so he doesn't feel threatened. Pulling out a huge fifteen-inch dildo could threaten a man who's not particularly confident about the size of his member, so perhaps you should pass over the John Holmes or Jeff Stryker look-alikes in lieu of something that more closely resembles his dimensions.

Now wouldn't it be nice if we could have molds taken of our lover's cocks so we could have an exact replica made? That should make him feel mighty special.

DIRECTOR'S NOTE

One of my pet peeves is a man who thinks the end of sex is determined by his orgasm. Think about it: you're really going at it, the man pumping away in a wonderful rhythmic pattern, both your pleasure levels climbing and climbing, and suddenly he spasms and comes and then stops. Meanwhile you're still climbing, or you *were*. And now you're supposed to just stop, immediately. There are times when I've had enough and the timing is fine. But there are others when it feels like coitus interruptus. I liken it to what guys used to call "blue balls," an agonizing condition they claim to suffer from after being stimulated and then having to suddenly stop. Well, perhaps it never occurred to them that women can feel the same way! My friend, sex coach Dr. Patti Britton, coined a great name for it, "pink belly." Believe me, I have suffered the same feelings men claim they feel from "blue balls": extreme frustration and at times even nausea. So I've learned to ask them to learn the art of finger fucking and the use of dildos and vibrators. After all, that's what after play is supposed to be all about, whether it's just gentle caresses and "I love yous," stimulating the woman to her orgasm, or gradually bringing the woman down through lesser and lesser degrees of penetration.

Talk Dirty to Me

Many a woman has confided to me that her lover wants her to talk dirty during sex. But most of these women are either uncomfortable with such talk, or just don't know how to do it. I've also had women tell me they wish their lovers *would* talk dirty to them. Let's tackle the issue of how to talk dirty first.

In order to be comfortable with this type of bedroom dialogue you need to know that there's nothing wrong or dirty about it. Speaking a little bit more pornographically doesn't make you a slut or a cheap woman. Talking dirty is just a natural expression of what's turning you on and what you'd like your lover to be doing, and that's how it should be approached.

Don't feel like you have to imitate those bad porno movies with the fake moans and groans and the trite clichéd exclamations like, "Ooh, you're sooo big" (men tend to disbelieve this even though their egos would like to) and, "Ooh yeah baby fuck me harder!" (though there could be a time and place for that too!). The simplest way to begin is to react to what you're feeling and to sort of describe what's happening. You can start with things like, "Mmmm, that feels soooo good," and "I love how your cock feels inside me." Then move on to, "Yeah baby, nail me to the bed!" and "Let me suck your swollen cock." Just let yourself go with what's happening and try not to edit yourself. And for heaven's sake, don't be shy. Lovemaking is one area where we are allowed to let our hair down and be the siren of our fantasies and the porn star of our own private movies. Nothing turns a man on more than seeing his woman get swept up in the passion of the moment and lose control of her otherwise prim and proper persona. So if he expresses a desire to have you talk dirty to him, just begin by expressing what's happening as if you're narrating the scene at hand. You might be surprised at how easily it can eventually come to you.

As for wanting your guy to talk dirty to *you*, I know I've found myself in that situation. I like when a man expresses himself this way. I can find out what sorts of things turn him on by these little comments and expressions that come out during the heat of passion, things like, "You make my cock so swollen," and "You need to be filled, don't you?" Obviously the first lover was turned on by the idea that a woman could make his penis become engorged and swollen with blood and make him lose control in a sense. The second comment reflects someone who's excited by the idea that a woman needs him to fuck her. These are all expressions of their own desires—the buttons that turn them on—and the added bonus of learning to bring out such a desire in him so that you can actually discover little secrets of what he likes in bed.

When I want to encourage a man to talk like this to me, I try to bring it out by talking to *him* during sex. "Do you like that?" I might begin in my sexiest throaty voice. "What would you like me to do to you? Tell me. How do you like it?" speaking not like a sex coach but a woman in the throes of heat and passion.

Talking dirty, or sex talk, is an art that can be learned. All it takes is a nonjudgmental and open attitude and a willingness to try. If it's something you both enjoy you will be amazed at how it can fire up an otherwise tepid erotic encounter.

Suggested Sex Dialogue

Remember, there are a few ways to come up with sex talk:

Describe What's Happening
> "Mmmmm, I like how your tongue's running along the lips of my pussy."
> "Ooh, I like how your cock feels inside me."
> "Your fingers feel so good down there."

Ask Him to Do Something in Particular
> "Yeah, squeeze my nipples."
> "Fuck me hard!"
> "Play with my ass."

Ask Him about What He Likes
   "Do you like that, baby?"
   "You like when I suck your cock?"
   "You want to fuck me now, don't you?"

Talking to Him About Erotic Movies

Introducing your desire to watch erotic movies can be just as daunting a task as bringing up the subject of toys. One way is to simply surprise him. I can't imagine a man who wouldn't thrill at the idea of coming home to a whole private sex orgy complete with sexy lingerie and an X-rated movie set up just for him.

But if you fear he might not approve, refer to it as something someone else mentioned, or something you read, like, "I was reading in such-and-such magazine the other day that a high percentage of couples today enjoy watching erotic movies together. What do you think of that idea?" This takes the onus off of you and puts it onto others, allowing yourself to get a read on how he might react to the idea.

As you read in chapter 3, there are many videos out there—so peruse the Web sites named in the resources section and select a couple that appeal to you.

Communication is vital to making any sexual relationship last; it's also vital to making it pleasurable. Do not think you can rely on intuition to figure out how your lover likes to be pleased. Pay attention to what seems to be turning him on and if you have any doubts or questions, ask. And don't wait for him to interview you about your desires and preferences. Show him through your responses and gently make suggestions while praising him for what he does well.

In the next chapter, you will (finally) take all the information you have gathered and put it to use. You will direct your body and that of your lover in your grand finale—the love scene to end all love scenes—that is until the next night!

Chapter 10

The Grand Finale

Sex pleasure in woman . . . is a kind of magic spell; it demands complete abandon: if words or movements oppose
the magic of caresses, the spell is broken.
—Simone de Beauvoir, *The Second Sex*

Goal-Oriented Versus Circular Sex

We've all watched films that seem predictable from the opening scene, and when this happens, we usually sneak out of
the theater or turn off the television. In my mind, sex that
is predictable is sex in which one or both partners is so focused on
the end result (intercourse and orgasm) that they barely stop for
pleasure along the way. Yet what happens along the way is the
essence of great sex. Think of the difference between a quick snack
at McDonald's or a meal at a five-star restaurant. At McDonald's
you slam your Big Macs down, suck in some french fries, and forget about the taste of anything a half hour later. In a fine restaurant, you and your lover linger over sensual appetizers, sips of
champagne, move on to a luscious soup with a dry white wine, delight in a sumptuous entrée accompanied by a deep red wine, finally indulging in a sweet rich chocolate confection or perhaps an
array of creamy rich cheeses and a fine port. You both enjoy every

course, relishing in the savory as well as the sweet. And though you feel wonderfully content by the dessert, it's the entire meal that completes and satisfies your appetite. The same applies to sex.

In this chapter, I offer you the crème de la crème of sexual tips and techniques that will rock your sexual world. I will explain how when it comes to being an expert lover, you must throw away the concept of foreplay—as all of sex is foreplay, play, and after play in an interchangeable round of delicious activities. I also offer tips on how to build up sensation and slow down your orgasm, and how to extend lovemaking all night long. By the end of this chapter, you will never again risk a night of predictable, goal-oriented sex!

Goal-oriented sex and *circular sex* are terms used in the sexual counseling community to describe different approaches to making love. Because we're a society driven by goals—whether they be in career, sports, or attainment of wealth—we have a strong mindset toward the end goal in most things we do. Unfortunately this all too often carries over into sex, with intercourse, and sometimes procreation, being the ultimate goal. Everything else we categorize as foreplay is seen as all leading up to that point. Generally the man's climax signals the end of sex, which can often leave the woman feeling less than satisfied at least, and extremely frustrated at worst. This linear approach to sex also often precludes a more open and creative approach to making love. It goes back to what I call "three-step sex": after some kissing the man fondles the woman's breasts, then he turns to the pussy, maybe some oral sex between the two, and finally the almighty act of intercourse.

Circular sex generally means sex that doesn't follow any set pattern and isn't led by any particular goal other than mutual pleasure and satisfaction. It may begin with kissing and sensual caressing, then it might lead to oral sex, and then a bit of intercourse. Then the couple might take a break from intercourse and go back to oral sex or the use of toys, maybe the woman's climax. Then they might return to intercourse, and so on. In other words, there's no set linear pattern, just a wonderful cornucopia of delicious things to do whenever it pleases one or both of you. This tends to allow for a greater and more creative range of sexual activity and one that is able to provide both parties with the pleasure and stimulation they need to be completely satisfied. It also takes the pressure off of men to have to hold out until the woman is satisfied. Once a man realizes he doesn't have to completely rely on intercourse to complete the act of lovemaking, he's free to explore and provide pleasure to his lover in a variety of ways without having to depend solely on his sometimes-fickle penis.

OUTERCOURSE SUGGESTIONS

These tips for prolonging outercourse can be used on either a man or a woman, unless otherwise directed.

- Lick and suck on your lover's earlobes; they can be *very* sensitive.
- Run your tongue along your lover's neck and gently bite it.
- Run your tongue around your lover's nipples and gently suck on them. Some men have very sensitive nipples and may even like having them lightly bitten.
- Trace your lover's body with your tongue.
- Massage your lover's inner thighs where they meet his groin, just brushing his genitals.
- Squeeze and massage the cheeks of his butt.
- Take massage to a new height by massaging every inch of your lover's body—without touching his or her genitals.
- Massage your lover's feet. It's said to be erotically stimulating to massage both big toes simultaneously.
- If you have long hair, sensuously run your locks along your lover's body, including his genitals . . . or ask him to do it to *you* if he has long hair!

Eliminating Foreplay

One of the first things we must do to break the pattern of linear goal-oriented sex is to throw away the concept of foreplay. This term presumes that everything is just the "presex" stuff that leads us up to the "real" sex. In goal-oriented sex, lovemaking becomes defined by the act of intercourse. A number of years ago, there was a movement in the sexuality field to embrace the concept of outer-course. Outercourse is about all the other delicious things there are to do *besides* intercourse. In fact this idea went so far as to urge people to explore the idea of sex completely without intercourse. While the concept of outercourse was already being discussed in the seventies, its renewed popularity was prompted by two things. One was the outbreak of HIV and the AIDS virus, and the need to get people to find ways to make love without intercourse. The other was the growing awareness of how we've come to define sex by the act of intercourse. This limited definition of sex, in fact, has even led in recent years to the troubling and growing number of young underage women providing oral sex to their boyfriends as an alternative to intercourse. Because they saw it as "not sex," this was done without the use of condoms and with the illusion that they were still "good girls."

Our limited view of sex as being solely based on intercourse has led most of us to fall into predictable patterns of making love that all too often preclude the notion of creative sexual exploration and the search for new and sensuous ways of pleasuring one another. It also continues to pressure men into thinking that their penises are their prime sources of providing satisfaction to their lovers. This often leaves the woman in need of more stimulation and afraid to ask for more for fear of hurting the man's pride. In addi-tion, an overreliance on goal-oriented sex all too often leads to the sexual rut of predictable sex so many couples find themselves in. A commitment to relearning and exploring new ways of making love can go a long way toward curing the well-known malaise of boredom in the bedroom and recharge an otherwise perfectly happy relationship. The first step in moving away from goal-oriented sex and toward an approach that is more circular is to rediscover your innate sensuality.

The Art of Sensuality

It is a loss of innocence and natural-born appreciation of sensuality that leads so many couples to the age-old troubling state of boredom. I became aware of this in my early thirties when I had already been married a few years. I had been feeling like something was missing from our sex life. I realized that I had completely lost touch with the wonderful phase of sensual exploration that I had so enjoyed when I was young and first discovering my sexuality. In the seventies when you met someone you liked it was as if all you did was say, "Hey, you're cute, let's fuck!" Then you'd go home together and basically, save for a few stops along the way, that's what we'd do: fuck. It's that "three-step sex": the guy plays with your tits, feels your pussy, maybe goes down on you, and then, voilà! You fuck!

You don't have to be a child of the love generation to have experienced this foreshortened version of sex. Having made my first boyfriend wait six months before I'd go all the way, we did a lot of making out and heavy petting. It turned me on enormously. I recall going home after a particularly long make-out session in his car and discovering an incredible wetness inside my vagina. I had no idea what it was and asked my older sister, who explained that that's what happens when a woman gets excited. (You can see how much sex-ed I got . . . I was already eighteen and didn't even know any of this!) Suffice it to say I was really enjoying all the touching and kissing and probing with fingers. But once my boyfriend got to deflower me, most of that delicious warm-up went the way of my virginity and it was down to the old three-step sex I came to know all too well. In other words, it's as if once we get permission to have intercourse, sex becomes defined by that act and it's that act that becomes the main event. Sensuality becomes something of the past, and we forget that our entire body is an erogenous zone.

Sensate Focus

When a couple seeks counseling for loss of desire, one of the most effective means of helping them rediscover their passion for each other is to help them relearn the subtle art of touching. Far too many people forget how wonderful it can be to just touch and be touched after years of going all the way. Relationship and sex therapists call this process sensate focus. According to the sex coach Dr. Patti Britton, sensate focus is a method that relies on using a focus on sensations to get away from mental anxiety. The following description of sensate focus is based on a program developed by Dagmar O'Connor, Ph.D., director of the sex-therapy program at St. Luke's Hospital Center in New York City, author of *How to Put the Love Back into Making Love* (Doubleday), and creator of a very moving video called *How to Make Love to the Same Person for the Rest of Your Life*, which was based on her first book of the same name.

For the first week the couple is instructed to take turns touching or being touched for about fifteen to forty-five minutes. The touchee lies passively as the toucher does nothing but softly touch and caress him or her. The next time it's the other's turn. But you can only touch, and you must restrict your touching to every place on the body except the breasts and genitals. And equally important, there is no intercourse or mutual masturbation allowed. The touchee gets to control where and how he or she wants to be touched by giving nonverbal signs, such as moving the toucher's hand and pressing it down for harder and up for gentler touching.

This is not a performance, and there is no right or wrong way to make moves. This interchange is also not considered foreplay, as it doesn't lead to anything. Instead, focusing on this kind of touching you can give—and receive—fantastic pleasure without the pressure to perform.

Dr. O'Connor tells the following story of one couple she worked with: a busy executive had always seen sex as orgasms with no sensuality, one for him and one for his wife, preferably squeezed into an occasional fifteen minutes before bedtime. During the first sensual exercise, he was acutely uncomfortable being touched by his wife and kept his eye on the clock the whole time, barely making it through fifteen minutes. By the fourth session, however, something happened. All of a sudden he started feeling exquisite sensations in his chest, belly, and thighs. When he opened his eyes he found he'd lost track of time for forty-five minutes. The secret, as Dr. O'Connor explains, is to focus on what you are feeling at the moment, without being rushed and without anticipating the next step.

During the second week, you continue your touching exercises, but get more creative with them, still avoiding the genitals, masturbation, and intercourse. This could include using a feather for stroking, licking your lover's neck, or rubbing scented oils on each other. O'Connor suggests experimenting with kissing. She points out that many couples abandon kissing over time because it's more intimate. In fact, O'Connor believes that one of the reasons many couples lose interest in sex is because it opens them up to the fears brought about by deep intimacy. In other words, wonderful sex makes us feel very close, as if we were merged with the other person. Although this intimacy might feel great at the beginning of a relationship, it can often become frightening as we fear losing ourselves in the other. Sensate focus addresses this fear as it helps people learn to let go while knowing they can regain control when they want to.

In the third week of sensate focus, couples are allowed to let genital sex back in, but in a whole new way. They are told to complete each session by masturbating simultaneously in front of each other. O'Connor explains that mutual masturbation typically causes barriers to drop away, allowing partners to seem more real to each other.

In week four, breasts but not genitals are included, but the touchee decides when and for how long so that the toucher cannot immediately dive for the breasts. O'Connor mentions that many men find for the first time that their nipples are as sensitive as a woman's. By week five, O'Connor has people do such exercises as standing before the mirror and looking at themselves, deciding what they like about their body; next, they do the same with and for their partner. They continue with mutual exploration of their genitals and show each other how they want to be touched. By week six, O'Connor explains that one should have learned that the key to deep intimacy is expressing your needs and the key to releasing your feelings is the ability to control them. By week seven, intercourse is gradually reintroduced. By this time you both should know your own body and your partner's well enough to know what pleases you both.

This is an elaborate process and perhaps not necessary for every couple. (For those of you interested in learning more, please refer to the aforementioned book and video, which I will also list in my resource guide.) But it might be worth your while to try a modified version of this process on your own to see what comes up as well as to slow down the act of lovemaking and learn how to focus on the wonderful sensations of lovemaking. Sensate focus is a way to wake up the whole body to feelings and sensations that we grow to rush past in our normal everyday approach to sex. It's the sexual version of stopping to smell the roses. And many a couple has rediscovered the wonder of one another's touch and rekindled their desire for one another at levels they never before felt. You might want to try your own abbreviated version of sensate focus by agreeing that you won't have intercourse for a certain number of encounters. Each of you can take turns being the "touchee" and the "toucher" and lay passively while your lover caresses you in a variety of ways while avoiding the breasts or genitals. The important thing is to come up with a plan and a timetable and to stick with it. You may be surprised at how sexy it can be to be forced to abstain from going all the way and by how many new and pleasurable sensations you might discover.

In regard to focusing on sensations, let me share a personal experience: some time ago when I was dating someone I liked, we had been out a few times and were only just getting to the point of smooching. We were sitting on my couch and he began to kiss me and softly stroke my arm. At first I was very nervous, and the usual thoughts were racing through my mind: *It's been several dates already . . . I'm sure he wants to begin getting physical . . . What if I don't like it? . . . What if he doesn't like me?"* etc., etc. Suddenly I realized how sensuously he was touching my arm and I said to myself, *OK, how about just focusing on his touch and how it feels?* So I did, and eventually my thoughts subsided and I got swept away in how wonderfully he caressed me. I realized that his touch was wonderful, and we ended up spending a lovely evening passionately kissing and sensually exploring each other's bodies.

My nervousness never returned and we went on to have a sweet, albeit brief, affair. Aside from the fact that this man did not turn out to be my next great love, I learned a very important lesson that night, and one that taught me the value of touch and sensitivity: by focusing on what I was *physically feeling* I was able to quell my thoughts and be in the moment. So the next time you find yourself feeling nervous with someone new, or your mind starts wandering to thoughts about what you have to do the next day when making love to your husband, remember to quiet your thoughts by focusing on the *sensations* you are feeling. This will put you right back to where you should be—in the moment.

DIRECTOR'S NOTE

Remember, becoming a sensual being requires that you be that way with yourself first. When you think of pleasuring yourself, whether it be with a vibrator or with your fingers or both, don't simply rush to your genitals. Let your hands glide along your body, notice how soft your belly feels, how smooth your skin is, and how your nipples grow as you become more excited. One of my favorite things to do when I first wake up is to run my hands along my body and softly stimulate myself awake—with or without masturbation.

I'll leave you with one last piece of advice about sensuous touch. In my adult life I've had two extraordinary lovers who I feel were my true passion match. One was the jazz musician who so creatively set up scenarios for me and would make love to me for hours and hours. The other, I'm happy to say, is the man I'm with now, who keeps me up for hours, devouring me in every which way. Both of these men have a tremendous appreciation for sensual touching that would go on for hours on end. And one of the things that my first perfect lover said to me explained what made him so outstanding. He told me that when he touched me, he wasn't just touching me; he was *feeling* me. He was feeling the softness of my flesh and the smoothness of my skin. He was feeling the curves of my hip and the roundness of my bum. He was truly feeling me, not just paying lip service to the idea of touching. And that I never forgot, because that is the essence of sensual touch, to really feel what you're touching.

When my boyfriend and I were first becoming involved, before we had even consummated our affair, he did the sexiest thing to me. It was our third date and we had already spent hours touching and fondling and kissing but hadn't yet gone all the way. We had now graduated to the bedroom and he maneuvered me onto my stomach and put his hand on the back of my neck and subtly began to hold me down as a lion grips and holds down his lioness by the neck. Then he began to ever-so-gently tease and caress my by-now sopping wet pussy, driving me wild with anticipation and desire. And again, he wasn't just gratuitously touching me there, he was *feeling* how wet my pussy lips were, taking great pleasure in knowing it was he who had gotten me there, and knowing all along that he was driving me wild with desire as he made me wait for the final moment. The combination of fierceness and sensuality drove me wild! I felt like his captive and I loved every minute of it.

Let Your Tongue Caress Him

One of the most frequently asked questions I get from women is how to give a great blow job. As I've already said earlier on, no two people are alike or like things done the same exact way. The best lovers are those who pay attention to their partner's responses in order to gauge what their partners seem to be enjoying, and especially those who simply ask what their lover likes. I will tell you what techniques I have found to work with almost any man.

○ Begin slowly and gently, almost teasingly in the beginning, with light caresses and gentle, teasing licks.
○ Lightly lick the head of his penis, paying special attention to just below the head, underneath the shaft where the skin comes together. This is a particularly sensitive area on a man's penis. Rolling your tongue around the head and then tickling this special area with your tongue is especially effective.
○ Lightly run your tongue up and down the shaft of the penis, beginning with the underside and eventually running your tongue along the entire shaft.
○ Eventually begin to take his penis into your mouth, sucking it in with your lips, being careful to avoid contact with your teeth. Teasingly start just with the head, and then gradually work your way down to enveloping the whole cock.

○ As you gently suck his cock up and down, be sure to maintain a steady rhythm. As he gets worked up it can be disconcerting to interrupt the feeling by stopping and starting.

○ You may want to gently wrap your hand around the shaft of his cock and move it up and down with the movement of your mouth. They should both go up and down together. Use your saliva as lubricant so it glides nicely.

○ Gently fondle his balls with your other hand. Then, while holding his erect cock with one hand, begin to lick his balls, at first teasingly with your tongue. Then very carefully take each ball into your mouth and lightly suck on it while running your tongue around it. Be very gentle and pay attention to his response. This is a very tender area for men. Some men love having their balls licked and fondled and sucked, while others find it too sensitive.

○ There is a tiny area between a man's balls and his anus called the perineum. This is a very sensitive area on a man and it can feel amazing to him if you lick it.

DEEP-THROATING

The late Linda Lovelace (Linda Boreman Marchiano) brought the concept of deep-throating to the world with her amazing skills. What many don't know is how she learned this skill. I happened to hear of this because I know a man who fought in World War II with her infamously abusive husband, Chuck Traynor. Traynor actually knew how to swallow swords and saw an opportunity in this. He later taught his wife, Linda Lovelace, the art of sword swallowing, knowing that the same principles could apply to swallowing any long object, as in an erect penis.

While you don't have to become a sword swallower to be able to take your lover's penis deep into your mouth, one principle that does apply is that of aligning your throat into one long, straight line and then concentrating on completely relaxing the muscles of your throat. I have found that if I position myself straight over the man's cock I'm able to pretty much get the whole thing into my throat, depending on how long he is. Another way is to lie on your back with your neck hanging over the edge of the bed. It helps to take a deep breath first since your man's penis will temporarily block your breathing. If you get the urge to gag, just swallow. With practice you can get pretty good at this and really wow your guy.

DIRECTOR'S NOTE
What Not to Do When Giving Oral Sex to Your Man

- Don't grab his cock and squeeze it like a vice! This is a tender area of a man's body and while some might like it rough, they usually still like to have it worked up to that point.
- While those who like it rough might also like you to use your teeth on them, gently raking your teeth along the shaft, most men cringe at the thought of feeling a woman's teeth on their cock. So be careful to use only your lips and tongue.

To Swallow or Not to Swallow

It's an unfortunate irony that while many women are brought up to feel disgust at the thought of swallowing a man's semen, men are completely ecstatic at the thought of it—hence all those porno scenes that end with the woman hungrily lapping up the man's come. It's the big forbidden fruit, the big fantasy for a man to have a woman *want* to swallow his semen. It shouldn't be difficult to understand his feelings. Think about how nice it is to know that he likes to lap up your juices and enjoys the taste of them. Think also about how awful it would be for him to say he was repulsed by the thought of licking and tasting you. Men are no different. If you're willing to try it, you'll make him mighty happy. For some women it's a nonissue. They're not only OK with swallowing their man's nectar, they're turned on by it. They're the lucky ones. Then there are others who have discovered such rewards for taking the plunge, so to speak, that they've become expert at it. One friend told me that her man was so grateful he became the most willing lover, spending hours on her pleasure, no matter what she wanted or how long it took! Here are a few ways to make it more pleasurable for you, as well as for him.

○ If you're ready and willing to swallow, be sure to have his cock as far back in your mouth as you can when he's coming and swallow it in one gulp, which allows the fluid to bypass the tastes buds. You will hardly know it passed through your mouth at all.

○ While some suggest holding the fluid in your mouth and politely excusing yourself to the bathroom to spit it out, I think this is a bit unnatural and can make him feel awkward. By leaving the scene, you still imply that you find the act of swallowing distasteful. The same is true of turning your head and spitting his semen into a tissue or something else nearby. If you're unable to tolerate the act of swallowing, what I've found works is to keep your mouth or lips lightly over the tip of his cock as he's coming and milk the shaft with your hand while letting the semen ooze out and down over his cock. This way you can also let the semen be part of the lubrication as you stroke his cock. Also, he might not even notice the difference between your saliva and his semen. Just the fact that you allow him to come (somewhat) in your mouth without gagging in disgust can make him feel very good. Obviously the best position for this is him on his back while you're over him.

○ If you *are* going to try and take a man's semen in your mouth, whether you swallow it or not, be sure to let him at least *think* you like the taste of it. There's nothing worse than feeling like your lover is disgusted by you or your fluids.

○ For your information, semen is utterly natural and harmless, comprised mostly of protein and sugar. There's nothing bad in it for you.

D I R E C T O R ' S   N O T E

If you are going to engage in oral sex and especially if you're going to take his semen in your mouth, be sure he's absolutely healthy and free of any sexually transmitted disease and especially of the HIV virus. Even if you just take his semen in your mouth, if he's infected it can reach your blood system by way of small cuts in the mouth or gums. Unless you've seen a clean bill of health, use a condom and forget about letting his semen anywhere near your mouth.

Tips on Getting Him to Taste and Smell Good

One of the stars in my movie *Stud Hunters* calls himself "Johnny Dannon" because of what he calls his "theory of yo." According to him, eating lots of yogurt will make a man's semen taste good. The same advice I give women for smelling and tasting good applies to men: eat lots of fruits and vegetables, lay low on animal protein, and drink lots of water. In addition, drinking too much alcohol will make both of you taste sour. So get your man to eat and drink well and the prospect of swallowing may seem that much less abhorrent. In fact, you might get him to eat healthier and drink less beer with the promise of such a reward.

What if you don't like the smell of your guy's genitals? This could also have to do with his diet and drinking habits. Perhaps you can subtly ease him into better dietary practices by offering to cook healthy meals for him. If you're not the cooking kind, suggest dining out in a healthier restaurant that serves fresh fish and vegetables. If the problem is with his personal hygiene habits, suggest an erotic bath or shower together before making love. Otherwise, you may have to have a heart-to-heart with him. I suspect that if you've gotten this far as a couple, and you're already considering ways to please him in bed, you probably do like his smell.

Research has shown that our personal scents play a major role in attracting each other. We're not even consciously aware of how much scent affects who we're attracted to. We've usually checked out one another's odors long before we've even stopped to chat. If we get as far as the bedroom with someone, chances are we're very into his smell. How many times have you had a man tell you, "Mmmm, I love how you smell," and he's not referring to your perfume! I love burying my nose in my man's neck and breathing in his personal scent. And every time I tell him how much I love how he smells he returns the compliment, telling me I always smell delicious to him. In this way we're very much like our animal friends. While each of us has a different standard as to how much we like our lovers to bathe and how much we like them to let their odors blossom, we're all finely tuned in to this very personal fragrance we each emit. It's said men can even subconsciously detect when women are ovulating by subtle olfactory clues. So don't worry about douching away your natural odors. Just practice good hygiene and hope he does too.

Here's a historical note: Legend has it that when Napoleon Bonaparte was returning home from battle he would send one of his couriers ahead to his love, Josephine, with the message, "Do not bathe. I am on my way home!"

It's Not the Meat, It's the Motion

When it comes to penis size, we've all heard the claim that size doesn't count. This opinion is oftentimes meant to assuage men's fragile egos—and in most cases it is true. The sexual power of a man lies in what he does with his penis and other parts of his body. My friend the ever-popular adult film star Nina Hartley has said more than once that she prefers a man with an average to just-below-average-sized cock. There are, however, times when the size of a man's endowment does count, and it's not just when it's on the small side.

I've probably received more inquiries over the years from women wanting to know how to handle their man's rather large member! Making love to a man who's very long can cause pain if he forcefully thrusts himself into you all of a sudden. Below are a few simple suggestions for dealing with a lover whose penis is below or above average:

○ Too long: Try making love from on top. This way you are in control and can regulate how deeply he enters you. When you want to be on the bottom try to keep your hips as low to the bed as possible. I have found that the more you lift your hips up, the deeper he will penetrate you, and forget about putting your legs up over his shoulders! Be sure to let him know to be careful so that he too can be mindful of not thrusting too deep or hard. Doggie style can be painful if the man is very long.

○ Too short: Here the opposite is true; try doggie style if your man's penis is on the short side. It allows the man to get deeper inside you.

○ Too thick: While there are women with serious problems that cause them to have difficulty opening up, this is not the norm. It's often caused by psychological issues or a rare condition that keeps the vaginal wall tightly clenched, which requires talking to a doctor or a counselor. Most of us, however, are quite able to accommodate a man of considerate girth; after all, our vaginas are constructed to allow a newborn baby to pass through. As a doctor once explained to me, the vagina is like an umbrella. It is full of folds and when necessary it's able to open itself wide enough to allow a baby to pass through—or, if necessary, a well-endowed man! John Holmes wasn't popular with the ladies for nothing! All you need to remember is to relax, breathe deeply if you need to relax more (just like with anal sex), make sure you're plenty turned on so you're well lubricated, and keep your favorite lube handy! As long as you're ready, relaxed, and well lubed, well, just consider yourself a lucky girl! Oops! . . . Oh yeah, size doesn't count!

The Anus and Men's G-Spot

While I will be focusing on anal pleasure for men here, if you are interested in being anally probed yourself, I would simply apply the same principles to yourself that I suggest when anally pleasuring your man. As I suggest below, you may want to begin with pleasuring yourself with a finger or butt plug to see how it feels and to practice relaxing and opening up. Learning to relax and open up is key to enjoying anal sex. There are a variety of books and videos that I list in my resources guide that can help you in this new exploration. You may want to read a book or view a video with your lover so that he understands how to properly do this without hurting or injuring you, thus making for a pleasurable experience for both.

Why does this area provide so much pleasure for a man? First of all, the opening, referred to as the anus, is rich with nerve endings. It's the stimulation of this area that brings much of the good sensation. Stimulating this alone, with either the tongue or the finger (watch those nails, girls!) can bring great pleasure. Just above the anus is the section called the rectum. While this area doesn't provide the greatest sensations, the man's prostate gland is located just in front of the rectum; its outline can be felt by inserting a finger through the anus and feeling the front part of the rectum. Stimulation of this area is said to provide amazing pleasure to some men. (In women, the structure in front of the rectum is the vagina, which is part of what can be stimulating for women during anal sex.)

Yet the anus is one area on the male body that evokes very different reactions in different men. I've experienced everything from lovers refusing to allow me anywhere near their delicate little opening to a past boyfriend who told me that once I orally caressed his anus he "knew I was the woman for him"! I even had a boyfriend who took out one of my Natural Contours Magnifique vibrators and, though I thought he was going to use it on me, he instead got lubed up and inserted it inside himself! This is one area where you absolutely need to be sensitive to where he falls on that scale. Just as women require tenderness when it comes to allowing something up inside their butts, so do men. And of course for men there is the very touchy issue of homophobia. For some men there's no fear of what it might mean for him to enjoy anal play, but for others this practice evokes strong fears or concerns about their masculinity. A woman needs to be sensitive to this and let him decide on his comfort level.

The bottom line is that this area can provide unbelievable pleasure for the man who's comfortable with it, as long as his partner is sensitive, gentle, and uses lots of lube. But be forewarned: playing with a man anally can also cause him to completely lose control and come before he wants to. It can feel that good!

The best way to assess whether your man enjoys or is open to anal play is to either ask him directly or pay attention to his response as you meander in that direction. Begin during oral sex by bringing your fingers closer and closer to his butt. You might massage the muscles of his butt, which can be very pleasurable without being threatening. Then begin to lightly run your fingers along the crack of his ass, getting closer and closer to his anus. Does he clench his cheeks tight? If so, that may be your cue to steer clear of that area. Does he arch his back or lift his hips up to meet your touch? Obviously he's telling you to carry on. If you feel comfortable enough, and if you feel confident that he's clean down there (again, an erotic shower or bath together might be in order for you to feel OK about going down there), sometimes the best way to begin is by gently kissing and then licking him there. The soft wetness of the tongue can be amazing for a man. If you're going to probe deeper, the important thing is to make sure he's well lubricated, either by your saliva or by a good lube. (Refer to the section on lubes in chapter 7.) Just as for women, men need to be probed carefully. Don't shove or push. Allow for the anus to open up bit by bit to your touch until you feel the sphincter relax. Then you can go further if you like. It's important for the person being penetrated to breathe deeply. This helps the muscles relax and open up. Again, be careful about your nails!

You may want to first play with toys made specifically for anal play, usually called butt plugs, though there are other variations. You'll want to heed the same cautions as if you were using your fingers. Use plenty of lube, go slowly, and allow time for the rectum to open up. The sex therapist and author Dr. Jack Morin, considered to be one of the leading teachers and authorities, explains in *The Better Sex Guide to Anal Pleasure* (Sinclair Intimacy Institute) that there are varying curves and directions that the rectum go in and that it might be good to begin by self-pleasuring with a finger or a butt plug to see what you like. This is obviously good advice for women looking to explore this form of sex play as well.

DIRECTOR'S NOTE

An important point about anal sex: don't ever feel like you have to do anything you're uncomfortable with. If this goes against what you're able to tolerate, don't feel like you have to. But if it's something your man likes and you're able to accommodate him, just like with any deeply intimate act, it will bring you that much closer.

Finally, with women taking more and more active roles and breaking gender stereotypes, it's no longer taboo for a woman to strap on a dildo and give it to her guy. The sex activist and educator Dr. Carol Queen produced and starred in a movie called *Bend Over Boyfriend* that sensitively explores the topic while showing how it's done. I tried it many years ago when I was in my twenties. My boyfriend at the time was very comfortable with his feminine side and sometimes enjoyed being able to be the one who was taken. One time in the heat of passion, I donned a strap-on and gave it to him. I must say it gave me a great sense of being in charge and it felt extremely liberating. I enjoyed the opportunity to feel what it was like to be the one on top, and he loved being able to be the passive one at my mercy. Even men who aren't the sensitive type can enjoy being anally taken. I had one woman express to me her surprise to discover that her terribly macho husband enjoyed having her strap on a dildo and give it to him. It often takes a man who's completely confident in his masculinity and sexual orientation to be open to exploring ways of being pleasured that might cause other men with less confidence to feel insecure.

Anal play is clearly not everyone's cup of tea and may be something you and/or your man has no interest in exploring. But if you think you might like to try this with your man, and he seems interested, be sure to be extremely gentle and employ good hygiene, extreme sensitivity, and lots of lube—just like you'd want done with you.

CANDIDA CLOSE-UP

Q: My boyfriend and I tried anal sex and I loved it. Doing it for several hours, on and off, I noticed that I began to come (anally). I never thought that was possible. Should I be worried?

A: Should you be worried? I don't think so! Anything that brings you such pleasure should be considered a good thing, as long as you're both being careful and responsible. In other words, the lining of the anal cavity is not nearly as sturdy as the mucous membrane lining of the vagina, therefore it is more likely to suffer small tears and abrasions. So you must make sure you're using plenty of lubrication and if you start feeling any pain, it may be a good idea to stop. The other important thing—*most* important!—is that you are both tested and are HIV negative. For the same reasons stated above, it is much easier to transfer the HIV virus to someone through anal sex. Be sure you're both tested and HIV negative or that you're using condoms that don't disintegrate with the use of lubricants. Silicone-based lubes tend to be the best as they stay slick and do not dry up, and they are also condom safe.

Becoming His Best Fuck

The first piece of advice I'd give is to stay active, exercise (your body *and* your vaginal PC muscles), and stay fit. Because I've maintained a regular exercise regimen that includes dance, yoga, calisthenics, and free weights, my body has remained strong and fit. As a result I have a lot of stamina, can get into all kinds of positions, and can make love for long periods of time. The downside is that I often can't be satisfied with men close to my age (forties and up) because so many of them let themselves go and are literally unable to keep up with me. They don't have the stamina or the strength to make love for very long or to be very acrobatic in bed. The same thing happens to women. One of the biggest compliments I've received from men is how much energy I have and how strong my body is. One lover told me few women can make love for very long, tiring easily and unable to take much.

DIRECTOR'S NOTE

For women dealing with the inevitable changes of perimenopause or menopause, there's been a lot of bad news about hormone replacement therapy (HRT) and its potential side effects. For those who want to stay sexually active this can be distressing news. A little extra estrogen and testosterone can do wonders to keep the libido strong and the vagina toned. Many women are not aware of the alternatives to standard synthetic HRT. Dr. Christiane Northrup talks about what are called bio-identical hormones in her wonderful book, *The Wisdom of Menopause*, and there are many practitioners who will do blood workups and prescribe them to those they feel will benefit from them. For a list of practitioners in your area contact the Women's International Pharmacy in Madison, Wisconsin, at 1-800-279-5708.

The second important piece of advice is to be open, creative, and versatile. Use imagination, be willing to try new things, and be open to making love in a variety of positions. And don't be afraid to climb on top. The *Kama Sutra*, a great reference guide for lots of different lovemaking positions, encourages you to "act the part of the man" and tells you, more specifically: "Lay him down on his back." Whatever is done by a man for giving pleasure to a woman is called the "work of man." So, in other words, do to your beloved what he does—or what you wish he would do—to you.

In addition, keep lots of lube on hand so you don't dry out before you want to stop, and if you want direct stimulation don't be too self-conscious to simply reach down and play with yourself. Most men enjoy seeing their woman letting loose and having a good time. It takes the pressure off them knowing she'll take charge of her pleasure and do what she needs to do to get off.

As for specifics, there's one thing in bed that I do that seems to really drive men wild, so much so that my boyfriend tells me I really should share this. Years ago I used to be too self-conscious about my body to want to have intercourse by riding on top of the man. Now that I've become more comfortable with myself, I know that a woman who's really into the sex is far more important to the man than how perfect her body is. Besides, as we women get older, we're more in touch with our own pleasure and able to abandon those silly fears for what just plain feels good.

As a result, I seem to have come upon a great way to fuck a man from on top. Rather than just trying to ride him by getting on my knees and sliding up and down his cock, I lower myself onto his cock and slide back and forth. The motion is like one of those old-fashioned lawn chairs that glides back and forth in one straight line. I don't lift up at all; I just rock my hips back and forth, starting gently but becoming very vigorous, never letting his cock slip out. It's a really strong movement that firmly grips and massages his cock.

I came upon this movement because it felt so damned good to me. It seems to get his cock really deep inside of me and massages lots of different sensitive areas in the vagina as well as really hitting the cervix. Of course you have to be careful not to hurt yourself. Sometimes the guy is too long for you, which might make this move painful. You also have to be careful not to hurt him. Make sure not to let him slip halfway out as you are moving; by doing so, you can bend the cock in a way it's not meant to bend, which would be very painful for him. You also have to be careful not to sit too far back as you can accidentally crush his tender testicles.

After I've had my orgasm I usually like to be fucked real good and I've found this is the best way to ensure a super good fuck. I just climb on and take charge! And he loves it—so much so that he often ends up coming this way. Most men just love the opportunity to occasionally lie back helplessly and be taken. My man looks luscious in this state. I'll often grip his arms and pin them back over his head like he does to me and just ride him until he can't take it anymore. He loves that I can give it as good as I can take it. And most men will agree that an active woman who's confident enough to really give it good to her man is a real turn-on.

Remember your kegels. There's nothing like a good tight pussy to grip your lover's cock and literally squeeze the juices out of him. Plus the stronger and better toned your vaginal muscles are, the stronger your orgasms. Remind your man to do *his* kegels too. The stronger and more toned the man's PC muscles, the longer he can hold out before coming and the stronger *his* orgasms! So do them together. Lie on your back and squeeze while he works his way up from lifting that measly little washcloth with his erect cock all the way to lifting a wet towel. Then go put that practice to good use in the bedroom!

DIRECTOR'S NOTE

Ladies, one way to encourage your man to do his kegels is by offering him some techniques. Try these on for size—pun intended!

○ Begin by helping your man get an erection.

○ Then have him use his erect cock to lift a dry washcloth.

○ Next have him wet the washcloth and repeat the exercise.

○ Next have him use a dry hand towel, then a wet hand towel, then a dry full-sized towel, and finally a wet full-sized towel!

Of course the real winner is the guy who can lift the large wet bath towel.

By now, any star lover worth her teddy might feel exhausted, and, I hope, fully satiated. But the fun is not over yet! In the next chapter you will see how you can get even more mileage out of your role as leading lady—just wait for those flashbacks to start rolling.

Phase Four

Postproduction

Chapter 11

Flashbacks

A Chinese poet many centuries ago noticed that to
re-create something in words is like being alive twice.
—Frances Mayes, *Under the Tuscan Sun*

Postproduction Play

One of my favorite aspects of postproduction is getting to view the footage I've shot. People often ask me, "Do you get turned on when you're shooting an erotic scene?" One might assume that to be the case; after all, I'm watching people make love right in front of me. But in fact, I don't really get turned on in the traditional sense—you know, tingly feelings down there, a gradual moistening, the desire to run to the bathroom and relieve myself. No, I have way too much to think about when I'm directing a movie: Will I get all the coverage I need? Will all the performers show up? Will they know their lines? Will they do a good scene for me? Will the guy be able to perform? Will we run into any unforeseen disasters? Who can possibly get off under those pressures?

What I *am* conscious of, however, is what looks good to me, what looks beautiful, and what is erotic. It's more of an intellectual knowing. I'm more aware of what's working in my head without necessarily feeling it in my groin, which would frankly be far too distracting for all I must concentrate on.

But when I am finally able to sit alone and view my footage, and relish in the erotic beauty of what I've captured on film or video, imagining how I can edit the footage and bring out the most in a scene, I sometimes have to take a break and relieve myself! It's during this delightful phase of making a movie, the editing phase, or postproduction, when I can see whether an erotic scene conveys all I want it to. When I'm brought to a certain sexual boiling point, I *know* I've got a good scene! I can't please all the people all the time, but if the scene at least gets *me* off, it's quite likely to get at least some other people off too.

Once I've pieced my footage together, gotten the film musically scored, and done whatever other technical work needs to be done, I'm able to sit back and truly enjoy the fruits of my labor. I'm usually able to bask in the satisfaction of a job well done, but often there are moments when I wish I might have done a scene differently, whether it be the script, the way I shot it, or how I chose to edit it. While it's too late to change anything once it's been completed, I will make a note to myself about what I'd like to do differently next time around.

Creating and reviewing an erotic movie is not unlike making love and later reviewing what you both did together. You and your lover have that same opportunity to admire and enjoy the fruits of your sexual experience when you come together outside of the bedroom (or whatever location you chose!) and recap the events of the night before. Not only do you reinforce what worked for you, but you also build up anticipation for the next encounter.

The Morning After

The first time I engaged in this type of discussion was with my first true passion match, the sexy jazz musician. It was after we had begun to really explore new avenues of sexual expression, engaging in frisky behavior neither of us had ever ventured into before. A whole new world was opening up to us now that we were taking turns surrendering to each other, and we found ourselves bursting and eager to talk about it. It was the morning after a particularly energetic night of adventurous lovemaking. I don't even recall who first brought up the subject, but once we began talking about our luscious night together, it felt completely natural and right. We discovered what we liked about the evening and what we might want to do differently as well as what we might like to try next time. Mind you, I was already thirty-eight years old when I first experienced this type of communication, and this is what's key here: it's all about communication.

We've all heard about how important it is to have good, clear, open communication in order for a relationship to work. Usually this dictum is in reference to an overall relationship, and applies to addressing unintended hurts or disappointments, or how to best discuss a problematic issue that's come up between you. Well, sex isn't any different. It's just as important to discuss your sexual issues as it is to discuss your overall relationship issues—that is, if you want a healthy, fulfilling sexual union that works for both of you. How can you possibly understand and know how each of you feels if you don't talk about it? For many, however, the problem is how to talk about it and when. Sex is a tough enough issue for many of us to broach. I've already talked about how difficult it can be to simply ask for what we like and need. Now we're supposed to talk about it after the fact and tell our partners what worked for us and what didn't? It can seem like an overwhelming task, but believe me, once you get the hang of it, it comes easier and easier and in fact it's even fun.

As I describe in chapter 9, there are moments during the act when it's appropriate to suggest something or to ask for it a little different, like, "Mmm, honey, that feels great . . . could you do it a little lighter?" or, "A little to the left," or, "I'd love it if you would put your fingers inside me while I play with myself." That's part of speaking up during sex in order to get what you need at the moment. What I'm describing in this chapter is more of a review, a recap for the sole purpose of getting to know each other sexually. This is the feedback stage where you find out what he liked and let him know what you liked, the postproduction phase when you get to look back on your erotic creation and learn what worked and didn't work so that you can make it even better next time. The ideal time to do this is *after* you're finished making love, though not necessarily right afterward, as if you've got your clipboard and you're just waiting to grade him on how he did. Maybe it's better to sleep on it, and then as you're lying in bed together after a bit of dreamy morning sex, or over Sunday brunch, you can begin to reminisce about your big night of lovemaking.

Talking about it the next day is like reviewing a wonderful movie you saw together. The best way to begin is always by complimenting your lover first. Even something as simple as, "Mmmm, honey, that was marvelous last night! I can't recall ever feeling that way!" Then you can move on to specifics. "I really loved when you inserted your fingers inside me while going down on me; it made my orgasm so much more intense." Another way to open up the flashback conversation is to ask him what *he* liked best. And remember, always start by saying something positive; you want to be as nonthreatening as possible in order to bring back the flush and euphoria of the evening. Then you can move on to something you might like done differently, which again can be put in a positive light: "The next time I'd love to see what it feels like when you leave your fingers in me a bit longer." This sets up the idea as something new to try and anticipate rather than a criticism. It says to him, "I want to make love to you again!"

Maybe there's something that didn't work for you or that you feel he should know. Again, as long as you begin with what you *did* like, he shouldn't be offended but rather will appreciate your willingness to share what you like and what doesn't work for you. No one wants to think he or she's doing something that doesn't feel good for you. Certainly this can feel a bit more awkward to bring up, but knowing it can only lead to better sex the next time should encourage you.

The other night my lover was so eager to try something new on me that he sort of sprung it on me before I was really ready and turned on enough. Not wanting to ruin the mood for him, seeing as this was extremely exciting for him, I decided not to say anything and simply go with it. Lord knows he's risen to the occasion when *I've* seduced him into sex even though he was tired from a hard day's work. However, the next day, while having one of our fun talks about the night before, I simply mentioned to him that next time I'd like to be a bit more warmed up before being introduced into such a fun new way of making love. While I was able to get into it and really liked it, perhaps next time he could help me prepare a bit more first. He wasn't at all bothered by this and completely understood. If you've established a good line of communication with your lover and you've both made each other feel confident and appreciated, this sort of request should absolutely not bother him. In fact a man who's willing and eager to please his woman would *want* to know this sort of thing so that he can be the best that he can be for her.

If you're still feeling insecure about bringing up this kind of reflection, perhaps the best thing would be to just be completely honest about what you're feeling. I have found that this really works for me. I will simply state the truth: "You know, I feel really silly about this, but I want to talk about last night and I'm feeling so shy about it . . ." There's nothing that touches people more than someone opening up and showing her vulnerability. I'll share an incident with you that took place a few years ago. While it wasn't a personal sexual experience, it illustrates well how being open about our insecurity can often be the best thing you can do in a certain situation.

Back in 1996, I was shooting my first feature in four years. Just like with stage performing and many other tasks, sometimes not having done it in a few years can really set you back and make you feel like it's the first time all over again. Even though I had already shot eight movies, the four-year lapse made me feel rusty and insecure about whether I could still do it. I was shooting in L.A. for the first time (all my other Femme movies were shot in New York), and except for just four people on my crew, all the others were strangers to me. Add to that the fact that at that time many people in the adult film industry still thought I had some sort of attitude, like I thought I was better than them. As a result I sensed that some of the people on my crew felt kind of like, "Well, let's just see what Ms. Royalle can *really* do," and were less than helpful as a result. This can be disastrous for a director. What you need is a crew that is respectful and eager to be there for you. I felt completely left in the lurch and things were not off to a good start. More than half the day had passed and we still hadn't gotten off one shot. I found myself beginning to get irritated and snapping at people. I knew this was not a good thing and would only further alienate them. And I knew I had to do something.

I took my four reliable crew members and called a meeting in another room. To my utter embarrassment I found myself completely breaking down in tears and admitting that I felt completely out of control of my crew and the situation and that I really needed them to rally around me and help me get through this. Somehow word of this spread throughout the rest of the crew and suddenly these guys couldn't do enough to help me. The rest of the shoot went fabulously and I completed my first movie in four years feeling confident and eager to do more.

I share this story because it illustrates how important and useful it can be to just be honest about what you're feeling. I'm not suggesting that you break down in tears over breakfast because you're feeling insecure about discussing your sex life with your lover, but I *am* suggesting that you be honest with him and let him know that you're feeling awkward and insecure and eager to talk. You'll be amazed at how that can break the ice. You'll also find that it somewhat disempowers those feelings of insecurity. Once you admit to them somehow their grip on you begins to dissipate. It's amazing how that works. Of course he might get scared and think you have something awful to tell him, so you might want to include in there that it's not that you have bad things to say, you just feel shy bringing up the issue of sex. Any healthy, loving man who truly cares about how you feel or what you have to say will encourage you and let you know he will not judge you for being open and honest about your sexual feelings.

I would again caution you *not* to approach sharing flashbacks as if it were an opportunity to critique his sexual skills, but rather a recap of how fun the sexual encounter was. Tell him what you liked, ask what he liked, and talk together about what you might like to do differently or in addition to next time. I really love when my lover and I talk about our sexual encounters. I'm always eager to know what he liked about them and I love letting him know what I liked. This back and forth gives me a real sense of being connected as well as a sense of sexual completion. I don't like wondering and playing guessing games about such things. I want to know if he's enjoying the same things I am, and I like letting him know how good he makes me feel. I also like letting him know when I need something else. Otherwise I will end up approaching our next sexual encounter with a sense of anxiety, maybe even dreading it because I'm afraid I won't like it.

I also like the quality of anticipation this kind of talk creates for us. It gets me revved up and eager for our next round of lovemaking. And I feel confident that it will be good, maybe even better, because we communicated about what we liked and didn't like. There were no loose ends, no misunderstood feelings. He knows I love what he does to me, I know he loves what I do to him, and we both know what we'd like to do differently next time.

And what if your man is reluctant to talk about it? Assure him that you adore making love with him (even if you have to exaggerate a little) and that it's all in the interest of making it even better and better. If you find that your talks end up going nowhere or that they become less than productive, or worse, contentious, perhaps you both need a little counseling in better communication skills. Again, I can't stress enough how important it is to be able to communicate your feelings with your partner, both general and sexual. Do not let a lack of communication develop between you. Every time you pull away in silence or secrecy is like adding another brick in the wall and you will end up with a relationship that is going nowhere. Relationships need to grow and evolve. Like water, they cannot stand still without stagnating. If you find yourself unable to talk to your partner you'd be better off finding someone to help you develop the communication skills to break through your impasse. I include a source for finding a good counselor in your area in my resource list at the end of the book.

Take Two

Now that you've created your first script and directed your first erotic movie, and you're done reviewing the footage and viewing it as a whole, you're ready to move on to your next great epic! The first movie is always the hardest. But with a bit of experience under your belt, along with the fact that you've broken the ice as well as recapped what you both liked and didn't like, you're even more prepared to direct the best personal erotic movie ever.

I have found as a director that not only does each time get better and better, I also come up with more and more ideas for the future. People often ask me, "Do you ever run out of ideas?" "Never," I assure them. The imagination is like a garden—keep feeding it and letting it blossom and it will forever provide for you. I have a file drawer full of ideas. Every time I get another idea, I scribble it down, make a folder for it, and file it away. When it comes time to do another movie, I open up my drawer full of ideas and search through it, discovering wonderful scenarios I had forgotten about. My movie *The Gift* came about that way. I had read about a man who, after his father's passing, had found and pored over all his father's old family albums. He discovered mysteries in these wonderful old photos and it led him to write about it in a book. I loved that idea and filed it away with the intent to one day direct a movie about a woman who comes across a family photo album up in a dusty old attic and discovers a secret that deeply affects her own life. When it came time to do a movie back in 1997, I went through my idea drawer and rediscovered that file. I was so excited at the thought of finally writing and directing that movie. Hence *The Gift* was born.

You too can file away your ideas. Maybe begin a fantasy journal where you jot down scenarios you'd like to create with your man. Maybe you can keep this journal together, discussing ideas for the next time you act out one of your own movies. Or maybe you prefer to keep it to yourself. That's up to you. You can even jot down the scenes you've acted out so you can go back and read them together. (Imagine growing old and gray together and rereading one of your personal erotic journals. Now *there's* an idea for a movie!) And the same way I make notes of what I'd like to do differently in terms of my next movie, you too can make notes of what you'd like to try the next time you direct your own private erotic scene.

The important thing is to feed and replenish your erotic imagination. For you will be feeding your erotic life and relationship with the man you love. He will adore you for it and you will ensure that your relationship never grows stale. The greatest act of love you can do is to nurture your private garden so that it forever blossoms and provides for you the fruits of your union.

Now go get that director's chair and get to work!

Acknowledgments

There are so many people who have been supportive and have helped me in so many ways, it would be hard to mention them all. First and foremost I'd like to thank my agent, Kim Witherspoon, who has for years remained supportive and encouraging as I figured out the "book that was in me." I felt a real kinship when we met and I was right. She's always been there for me. I also want to thank my editor, Cherise Davis, for her enthusiasm, guidance, and terrific positive spirit. And Billie Fitzpatrick, my collaborator. I couldn't have asked for a nicer, more solid and capable person to help guide me through my first book. Thanks also to Alexis Hurley for her help and assistance.

I want to thank Marcella Landres, whose eager enthusiasm and interest in my book helped get it published. Her early guidance was invaluable. And my friend Judy Farkas, whose belief in me all those years ago got the doors opened to the many agents I met with, and most important, to Witherspoon and Associates.

Many people helped me get where I am now. My ex-husband and eternal friend, Per Sjöstedt, offered his love and support back when I was most vulnerable and in need of a stable, loving home front. I want to thank him and his father, Sture Sjöstedt, for believing in me enough to finance my fledgling film company, Femme Productions, an idea way ahead of its time. My original partner Lauren Niemi Cole's early vision magically blended with mine, resulting in the creation of Femme Productions.

Thanks to everyone at PHE, Inc., for their belief in me and my work; especially Phil Harvey for his vision, work, and personal sacrifice in the name of a sane and intelligent society regarding sexuality and the freedom to access sexual materials; and to Bob Christian for his professional support and a friendship I know will live beyond our professional relationship. Kitty Speelman and Jandirk Groet, my partners in Natural Contours, brought to me not only an opportunity that was brilliant, timely, and ultimately tremendously successful, but also showed me that you can be business partners and incredible friends at the same time; Susan Montani's professional skills have helped make our ideas a major success. Monika Napolean's good work for me is eclipsed only by the deep regard I hold for her. She has been like a mother to me and her spirit and zest for life in the face of incredible challenges have been an enormous inspiration to me. Thanks to Suzanne Delaney, whose kindness and loyalty have meant so much to me.

I have to mention my sisters in Feminists for Free Expression (FFE), especially founder and former president Marcia Palley, Ph.D.; former vice president Joan Kennedy Taylor; and current president Mary Dorman, J.D. This has been an amazing group of women whose faces have changed through the years but whose purpose and determination has never wavered.

Thank you to my sisters in Club 90. When one speaks of family, no group of women could fit that description more than you. Move over Carrie Bradshaw. We were doing it years ago! Veronica Vera,

Annie Sprinkle, Veronica Hart, and Gloria Leonard . . . it's been twenty years and we still turn to each other for love, guidance, support . . . and fun!

Then there are the many friends who have been there for me in so many ways: Michele Capozzi, who has been my biggest cheerleader, confidant, and professional collaborator; Roger Hines, whose love, friendship, and good humor have comforted me in so many ways as well as his tremendous professional help; Dianne Stasi for her generosity in both friendship and professional work; Dr. Patti Britton, who's been both a wonderful friend and a fun professional collaborator; Dr. Diana Wiley for her friendship, encouragement, and support; Dr. Sandra Cole for her support when I was a fledgling erotic filmmaker. It was she who brought me into the world of sexology during her tenure as president of the American Association of Sex Educators, Counselors, and Therapists, inviting me to speak to and address this community, and ultimately to join in as a peer, a move whose professional repercussions have been immeasurable. Nadine Strossen, president of the New York Chapter of the ACLU, for both her support and her recognition of my work and for her incredible efforts toward free speech and liberty; and Nancy Friday, for the important work and ideas she's expressed in her many books, her support of women's sexual lives, and her generous recognition of my work.

I cannot leave out my family, whose acceptance of my unconventional profession has meant so much to me, especially my sister, Cinthea, for her loving support, enthusiasm, and undying friendship. And while they're no longer here to read this, I must thank my mother and father for their love, encouragement, and, indeed, their acceptance of my life choices.

I want to thank the many men and women who have shared their own personal stories and secrets with me. Your stories have helped shape what I do and say through my work. And your thanks and comments about my work have helped get me through the tough times. You have no idea how much it means to me to hear that what I have done has touched so many.

Finally, I want to thank Larry Trepel, whose love and passion gave me new inspiration with which to write this book. I only dreamed that love could be so easy. I never thought I would meet my perfect mate so well into my adulthood. You have given me so much.

Resources

Ⓞ

Web Sites and Catalogs

Because so many of the following Web sites and catalogs have varying and overlapping offerings mentioned throughout my book, I list them here in no particular order and describe what you can find in each one.

Candida Royalle
CandidaRoyalle.com
800-456-LOVE (5683)
Natural-Contours.com
For info on myself, my work, and my Femme line of erotic adult movies from a woman's point of view and my Natural Contours line of ergonomically correct sexual products for women.

Adam & Eve
AdamEve.com
800-293-4654
A wide variety of movies and toys, including my Femme line of "woman-friendly" erotic movies, the Ultimate line, and Nina Hartley's line of informative and sexy how-to videos about all sorts of sexual techniques and practices, from *Nina's Guide to Sensual Domination* and *Nina's Advanced Guide to Oral Sex* to Nina's Anal Sex Kit, complete with instructional video, lube, and her favorite toys. Nina Hartley is a highly popular adult film star and sex educator. Learn more about her at Nina.com.

Sinclair Intimacy Institute
Bettersex.com
800-262-7367
High-quality, sensuous instructional videos covering many topics,
from erotic massage to sensuous role-playing to anal sex. The site
also offers great info, including "Sexuality Encyclopedia," a resource list and lists of questions answered by their director of sex
education, Mark Schoen, Ph.D.

Dagmar O'Connor, Ph.D.
DagmarOConnor.com
Dag Media Corp.
800-520-5200
I found Dr. O'Connor's book and video, both called, *How to Make
Love to the Same Person for the Rest of Your Life,* incredibly inspiring.
Includes a description of her sex therapy program and her applica-
tion of the technique called "sensate focus." Her newest video is
called *Sharing Yourself with Your Lover.*

Patti Britton, Ph.D.
Yoursexcoach.com
Dr. Britton, board-certified sexologist, has an upbeat Web site full
of helpful information and reviews of products. She also has a
unique style of counseling called "Sex Coaching."

Marty Klein, Ph.D.
Sexed.org
A great thinker who offers "straight talk on sex, love, and intimacy" on his site as well as the many excellent books and articles
he's written, along with CDs and audiotapes and even a Q&A section.

Access Instructional Media
SexualIntimacy.com
Dr. Michael Perry's line of erotic instructional videos, featuring at-
tractive people and many topics. Of special interest is *The Amazing
G-spot.*

LouPaget.com
For the Lou Paget collection of popular books on sex and relationships, including *How to Be a Great Lover* and *365 Days of Sensational Sex*.

Tantra.com
800-9-TANTRA
Both sensuous and educational videos and books that are "innovative, fun, enlightening, educational, spiritual, and sexy," related to tantra and sacred sexuality.

Loveandintimacy.com
800-262-7367
A good selection of video programs on couples intimacy, erotic massage, erotic dancing, sexual fantasy, and other aids to intimacy.

AnnieSprinkle.org
Annie Sprinkle is well known for her colorful career as an adult film star and more recently as a performance artist and teacher of sacred sex. Her site is full of her knowledge and personal views on women's sexuality, orgasm, and other political and controversial topics, and offers the many books she's written and videos she's produced and directed.

BettyDodson.com
Betty became known as the "mother of masturbation" for her wonderful workshops on "self-loving." Her site offers advice along with the many books and videos she's done, my favorite being *Self-Loving: Video Portrait of a Women's Sexuality Seminar*.

MissVera.com
This official site for "boys who want to be girls" is of special interest for wives and significant others whose man "loves to wear a dress," otherwise known as cross-dressing. Both the site's "Wives & Partners" page as well as Miss Vera's latest book, *Miss Vera's Cross-Dress for Success: A Resource Guide for Boys Who Want to be Girls*, have good info for women.

BarbaraCarrellas.com
Barbara conducts workshops on "Urban Tantra," based on her book by the same name, for "those who live in intense urban environments." She has created a unique blend of tantra and S&M.

JadeGoddess.com
604-731-4835
I don't know this woman personally, but I hear great things about her many workshops on Taoist practices, qi gong breathing techniques, and other spiritually infused sexuality practices.

TantraNewYork.com
Tantra teacher Carla Tara's site with her own personal teachings on tantra as well as videos, sex aids, and workshops in New York and Maui.

Books

Cleis Press
CleisPress.com
800-780-2279
415-575-4700
Lots of interesting and informative books under "Sex Guides," including the *Ultimate Guide to Adult Videos*, books about submission and domination, lesbian sex, and *How to Have an Empowered Sex Life After Child Abuse*.

Of special note:
The Wise Woman's Guide to Erotic Videos: 500 Sexy Videos for Every Woman—and her Lover, by Angela Cohen and Sarah Gardner Fox (Broadway Books).
Includes Hollywood films, classics, foreign, educational, and adult films.
Getting the Sex You Want: A Woman's Guide to Becoming Proud, Passionate, and Pleased in Bed, by Sandra Leiblum, Ph.D., and Judith Sachs (Crown).
Two leaders in the field of female sexuality give great advice for

women of all ages looking to recapture their desire and attain the good sex they're entitled to.

The Wisdom of Menopause: Creating Physical and Emotional Health and Healing During the Change, by Christiane Northrup, M.D. (Bantam Books).
A wonderful book for women either entering or going through menopause.

The Ultimate Guide to Adult Videos: How to Watch Adult Videos and Make Your Sex Life Sizzle, by Violet Blue (Cleis Press).

Guide to Getting It On!, by Paul Joannides and Dærick Gröss (Goofy Foot Press).
A fun, informative, and sexy book illustrated with delightful comic-book type drawings that will appeal to adults of all ages, including college age.

Dr. Sprinkle's Spectacular Sex, by Annie Sprinkle (Tarcher/Penguin).
A delightful, unique, and upbeat guide to getting the sex you want based on the legendary Annie Sprinkle's vast life experiences and years of human sexuality research.

The Good Vibrations Guide to Sex, by Cathy Winks and Anne Semans (Cleis Press).
Lots of great information and illustrations!

The Complete Idiot's Guide to Sensual Massage, by Dr. Patti Britton and Helen Hodgson (Alpha Books).
Valuable stuff!

Sex Matters for Women: A Complete Guide to Taking Care of Your Sexual Self by Sallie Foley, Sally A. Kope, and Dennis P. Sugrue (Guilford Press).
A wonderful book!

Erotica

LibidoMag.com
800-495-1988
This "Journal of Sex & Sensibility" is an online magazine of high-quality erotic photographs, fiction, humor, news and essays, a calendar of erotic events, reviews, even a new art museum. Also

available are their own couples-friendly videos, a good alternative to commercial porn.

ScarletLetters.com
Woman-owned and -run "sex-positive webzine" of erotica, visual art, prose and poetry, nonfiction, and an interactive forum.

Lingerie, Sexy Costumes, and Fetish Wear for Regular and Plus-Size Women

Secrets in Lace
Secretsinlace.com
877-373-5223
Wonderful lingerie and great stockings. Special "Curvy Women" section for plus sizes. Personally endorsed by my friend Ms. Veronica Vera, who loves their retro and seamed stockings and thigh-highs for plus-size women.

Trashy Lingerie
Trashy.com
310-659-4550
Based in Los Angeles. I used to buy lots of fun, racy, and hip lingerie here.

Ms. Antoinette's Versatile Fashions
VersatileFashions.com
714-538-0337
Specializing in fabulous high-quality, custom-made corsets and fetish wear. All sizes, even for the transgendered! Made to order.

Agent Provocateur
AgentProvocateur.com
Fabulous and fun cutting-edge lingerie with a touch of retro and fetish. Retail boutiques located in London, Los Angeles, and New York City, where it's perfectly designed for men to accompany you and have you model the selections.

La Petit Coquette
TheLittleFlirt.com
212-473-2478

This small, elegant boutique based in New York City has some of the loveliest European designer lingerie you'll find. Also has a place for your man to watch you model your selections. My boyfriend's favorite place to shop for me!

StormyLeather.com
All sorts of stylish fetish wear, including nonleather, vinyl, and latex. Even has plus sizes.

VeganErotica.com
Sexy, cruelty-free synthetic sex toys made from sleek black "pleather" imported from Italy, a lubricant that's safely tested without harming animals, and S&M playthings.

Wolford
WolfordBoutiqueLondon.co.uk
Some of the best-quality and most sophisticated lingerie available, with boutiques in many cities in the United States and Europe.

Upon checking, I found *sooo* many sites that cater to the more curvy woman on the Internet. Just Google "plus-size lingerie." While I haven't ordered from any of them, the following looked especially interesting to me:
Lingeriesite.com
888-434-4488

Flirtylingerie.com
877-354-7895

HipsandCurves.com
Has sections for erotic reading, a newsletter for seduction tips, and a photo gallery featuring their "full-figured customers."

HerRoom.com
800-558-6779
More subtle lingerie for everyday and evening wear. Good info about basics, and for those who care, what the celebrities are wearing, like Oprah's favorite bra and Renée Zellweger's favorite low-rise hip G-string.

Referrals and Information Regarding Sex and Marital Counseling

American Association of Sex Educators, Counselors, and Therapists (AASECT)
AASECT.org
Listings of certified sex therapists and counselors based throughout the United States.

Institute for Marital and Sexual Therapy
SexualTherapy.com
Directory of therapists, related links, even offers online therapy for fifty dollars per "valid" question. Includes a listing for Dean Dauw, Ph.D., in whose book *The Stranger In Your Bed: A Guide to Emotional Intimacy* I learned about the "give-and-get" method mentioned in chapter 5.

Marriage and Family Health Center
PassionateMarriage.com
303-670-2630
Founded by Dr. David Schnarch and Dr. Ruth Morehouse, for couples, relationship, and sexuality enhancement courses, including "Passionate Marriage" couples' retreats and couples' enrichment weekends.

For Women Interested in Finding Practitioners Experienced in Natural Hormone Replacement

(also known as "bio-identical hormones")

WomensInternationalPharmacy.com
Under "Resources," "Practitioner Referral"
800-279-5708

Women-Friendly Retail Erotic Stores

Women- and couple-friendly erotic shops are popping up everywhere, therefore it's impossible for me to include all of them, but here's a list of some of the more established ones that I know of. Most of these stores also have Web sites and mail-order catalogs.

Eve's Garden
119 West 57th Street
New York, NY 10019
800-848-3837

Toys in Babeland
707 E. Pike Street
Seattle, WA 98122
206-328-2914

Also:
94 Rivington Street
New York, NY 10002
212-375-1701

And their spiffy new one in
SoHo, New York:
43 Mercer Street
New York, NY 10012

Ruby's Pearl
323 E. Market St.
Iowa City, IA 52245
319-248-0032

A Woman's Touch
600 Williamson St.
Madison, WI 53703
608-250-1928

Good Vibrations
603 Valencia Street
(at 17th St.)
San Francisco, CA 94110
415-522-5460
Call for additional locations
in San Francisco and
Berkeley, CA.

Grand Opening!
318 Harvard Street, Suite 32
Brookline, MA 02446
617-731-2626

Adam & Eve
6311 Glenwood Ave.
Raleigh, NC 27612
1-919-571-7209
Visit AdamEve.com/stores
for listings of additional
locations in Winston-
Salem, Charlotte,
Greensboro, and Durham.

Hustler Hollywood
8920 Sunset Blvd.
West Hollywood, CA 90069

Early to Bed
5232 N. Sheidan Rd.
Chicago, IL 60640
1-773-271-1219
(Sex toys only, no movies)

G Boutique
2131 N. Damen Ave.
Chicago, IL 60647
773-235-1234

Wildflowers
1407 N. Wells (Inside
"Gaslight Courtyard")
Chicago, IL 60610
312-654-0482

Free-Speech Groups

Feminists for Free Expression (FFE)
FFEUSA.org
718-651-1232

National Coalition Against Censorship (NCAC)
NCAC.org
212-807-6222

Free Speech Coalition
FreeSpeechCoalition.com
818-348-9373
Toll Free: 866-372-9373

Index